THE MASTER ARTIST

Finding Healing for Your Heart
through the Ministry of His Heart

PRISCILLA MUÑOZ

WESTBOW
PRESS®
A DIVISION OF THOMAS NELSON
& ZONDERVAN

This book is a work of non-fiction. Unless otherwise noted, the author and the publisher make no explicit guarantees as to the accuracy of the information contained in this book and in some cases, names of people and places have been altered to protect their privacy.

WestBow Press books may be ordered through booksellers or by contacting:

WestBow Press
A Division of Thomas Nelson & Zondervan
1663 Liberty Drive
Bloomington, IN 47403
www.westbowpress.com
844-714-3454

Because of the dynamic nature of the Internet, any web addresses or links contained in this book may have changed since publication and may no longer be valid. The views expressed in this work are solely those of the author and do not necessarily reflect the views of the publisher, and the publisher hereby disclaims any responsibility for them.

Any people depicted in stock imagery provided by Getty Images are models, and such images are being used for illustrative purposes only. Certain stock imagery © Getty Images.

Unless marked otherwise, all Scripture quotations are taken from The Holy Bible, English Standard Version® (ESV®), Copyright © 2001 by Crossway, a publishing ministry of Good News Publishers. All rights reserved.

Scripture quotations marked NKJV are taken from the New King James Version®. Copyright © 1982 by Thomas Nelson. Used by permission. All rights reserved.

Scripture quotations taken from the (NASB®) New American Standard Bible®, Copyright © 1960, 1971, 1977, 1995, 2020 by The Lockman Foundation. Used by permission. All rights reserved. www.lockman.org

ISBN: 978-1-6642-1449-1 (sc)
ISBN: 978-1-6642-1448-4 (hc)
ISBN: 978-1-6642-1450-7 (e)

Library of Congress Control Number: 2020923885

Print information available on the last page.

WestBow Press rev. date: 02/11/2021

Contents

Dedicated to my sisters.

Stephanie, thank you for always being a voice of
encouragement, acceptance, and hope in my journey out
of darkness into light. He has made everything beautiful
in its time. Vanessa, Stacey, Kristine, Ashley, and Amber,
God's love for you is deeper than the ocean itself.

Thank you, Merlie Huey, for all of your prayers, support, and
encouragement. I love you and am eternally grateful for you.
Yo'EL, I am so thankful to God for you. He is the Master Artist!

Introduction

He has made everything beautiful in its time. Also, he has put eternity into man's heart, yet so that he cannot find out what God has done from the beginning to the end.

—Ecclesiastes 3:11

The Holy Spirit ministered to my heart through art during a transformational season of my life. During this period, I learned that I had a tough time submitting to my own Artist—God. He promised me that I was part of His masterpiece, but I found it difficult to trust and obey Him. In my creative yet hurting heart, I felt broken, undeserving, and distrusting of His love for me. My heart felt shattered inside. Because of past experiences, my heart was wounded, bitter, ashamed, and angry.

I am sure this is a common state of many hearts in the world. I didn't know how I could ever change and move beyond my past. I claimed to love Jesus because of what He did for me on the cross, but it was challenging for me to move forward in my walk with Him. Perhaps your heart is in the same place. Your heart might not know how to get up and walk. Your heart might be fearful of the future, as it has only known darkness up until now. Your heart might feel discouraged, as it does not yet know the redemptive character or voice of God.

The purpose of this book is to minister to the souls who feel broken inside and help them in their journey towards wholeness in Christ.

Little by little, the Father's love drew me to repentance from my sins, helping me die to self and live to His Son, Jesus Christ. His love turned me from the power of Satan to the power of God, from darkness to light, so that I might be sanctified by faith in Him (Acts 26:18). Today, it is no longer I who live but Christ who lives in me. And the life I now live in the flesh I live by faith in the Son of God, Who loved me and gave Himself for me (Galatians 2:20).

The ministry of God's beautiful Heart healed my captive, lost, and broken heart. He has made me into a new, sanctified vessel for Himself, able to reflect His light to others. If God did this impossible heartwork in me, He can do it for anyone willing to submit to Him as their Artist. Through this book, I would like to share with you the truths the Lord ministered to me during this season of my life. I pray that as you come out of darkness and into His marvelous light, you will begin to see, enjoy, and reflect His beautiful Heart for you and all of creation. I pray that like a butterfly, in His timing, you will be able to display the colors of His Heart to everyone around you. This is what we were made for: to be in sweet fellowship with our Maker.

The Artist and His Heartwork

The Bible says that God is good (Psalm 136:1). "Good" in this scripture comes from the root word towb in Hebrew.[1] It means that He is morally good in nature, kind, upright, and generous. He is faithful from eternity past, today, and forever.

This is God's character: good.

In Genesis 1:1, we learn that God created the heavens and the earth. The word "created" in Hebrew is *bara*.[2] Out of nothing, God created, shaped, and formed His creation. He made the stars, seas, and creatures. The heavens and the earth, the animals, and the stars were also made to display His glory. Can you imagine what these creative acts must have looked like? Incredible! Like Him, everything God made was very good.

> And God saw everything that he had made, and behold, it was very good. And there was evening and there was morning, the sixth day (Genesis 1:31).

God is a good Creator Who makes good things.

---

[1] https://biblehub.com/hebrew/2896.htm
[2] https://biblehub.com/hebrew/1254.htm.

God made humans in His own image. Genesis 2:7 says, "Then the Lord God formed the man of dust from the ground and breathed into his nostrils the breath of life, and the man became a living creature." "So God created man in his own image, in the image of God he created him; male and female he created them" (Genesis 1:27). The first man, Adam, was made from the dust of the ground. The first woman, Eve, was made from Adam's rib. Distinct from the rest of God's creation, Adam and Eve could think, reason, and even love God and each other. They were made with the ability to exercise their own free will. For a time, life in the Garden of Eden was wonderful—good. "And the man and his wife were both naked and were not ashamed" (Genesis 2:25).

Here we are affirmed: God is good.
God is the ultimate Creator and Artist of all creation.
Everything God made was good.
Essentially, God's Art reflected Who He is; His good nature.

In modern-day culture, art normally reflects an artist's heart and mind. The paintings and designs we create leave our unique marks and handprints on them. Think about some of the artwork that is showcased in the world today. No piece of art is an exact replica of any other artwork. Twenty artists can be in the same room working on the same painting, and what they each produce will be distinct from the others. This is because the art we make derives from our individual hearts and minds.

God's Art was made in His likeness and was created to reflect His image (Genesis 1:27). We were created to demonstrate who our Artist is—good. Males were made to be different from females, and each of us was made to uniquely express God's character. "He created them male and female, and blessed them and called them Mankind in the day they were created" (Genesis 5:2 NKJV). Women were created to give life, and men were created to protect life.

This was God's intention when He made His creation—good.

Why then do we see so much evil in the world? Mass shootings, bullying, suicides, racism, pandemics, and so on? These acts against humanity do not seem to reflect our Artist's heart and mind. They certainly do not display His good character. The news we watch or read about echoes desperate cries of hate, sorrow, and despair. The realities of our world hit the core of our souls when we learn that people are murdered for no apparent reason. Healthy businesses are robbed. Families are destroyed. Communities are demolished.

Many of us do not even need to watch or read about this news to know that evil exists. It could be transpiring in our homes right before our eyes. Perhaps we were born into or grew up in such a setting. For some of us, larceny, thievery, and divorce touched our parents' lives before we knew what harmony could look like in a household.

Today, the good we long for in our hearts does not always align with the reality of our lives or the lives in front of us.

The Bible says that though humanity is God's Art, we come into this world separated from Him. The word "separated" in Hebrew is *badal*, which means to be divided, separate.[3] Psalm 51:5 says, "Behold, I was brought forth in iniquity, and in sin did my mother conceive me." Born in the flesh by your mother, you are introduced to a world that seems foreign. It is new and appealing to your senses. Yet it drives you to seek comfort from another place—a home base. The closest dwelling to soothe your heart's cries is your mother's arms. Yet not even her arms can meet your innate need to be united with God Himself. Separation from God, if not already present in your physical home, exists within your heart from the time of conception.

---

[3] https://www.biblehub.com/hebrew/914.htm.

God's Word indicates that we are separated from God by our sin. Sin is defined as a transgression of the law of God.[4] We as human beings naturally miss God's ultimate standard of goodness, and we sin against God in our hearts. We are born with rebellious hearts, and these hearts lead us astray, away from God. Sometimes they hurt others (or ourselves). Sometimes they deceive us and bring us to places we never imagined we would go. "The heart is deceitful above all things, and desperately sick; who can understand it?" (Jeremiah 17:9). Isaiah 59:2 says, "But your iniquities have made a separation between you and your God, and your sins have hidden his face from you so that he does not hear."

In our sins, we remain separated from our Artist. Our hearts are blind and deaf to our Maker and His goodness. We cannot see God's light, beauty, and love. We cannot hear His good and peaceful thoughts toward us (Psalm 139:17–18). Without Him, our bodies are full of darkness (Matthew 6:22–23). In our sins, we walk around the world in rebellion against God. Apart from Him, we do not know where we are going or what our purpose is on earth. Our hearts go where they will, far away from our Artist. They can even head toward hell and think they are on the right path (Proverbs 16:25).

This is the condition of much of creation today. The hearts of men and women are at war against God. These hearts partake in deeds of darkness that hurt us and others around us. Without God, we are destructive—even in our best efforts to perform good works. "We have all become like the one who is unclean, and all our righteous deeds are like polluted garments. We all fade like leaves, and our iniquities, like the wind, take us away" (Isaiah 64:6). This is because sin, rebellion against God, occurs within us, where He sees.

Sin breaks, divides, and destroys God's creation, and this grieves His Heart tremendously. He hates sin because it leads us astray and takes us away from Him and His ultimate purpose for us. The result of sin

---

[4] https://www.merriam-webster.com/dictionary/sin.

against God and one another is death. Romans 6:23 says, "For the wages of sin is death, but the free gift of God is eternal life in Christ Jesus our Lord." This is the reason death lurks behind the voices of reporters sharing sad news on television—murders, robberies, and divided families. They provide a picture of sin in the world.

How, then, did creation separate from its Artist? How did sin and darkness enter the world? Why is God's image in humans so marred today? The Bible says that humankind fell into sin in the Garden of Eden, where the first man and woman, Adam and Eve, were placed (Genesis 3). Adam and Eve uniquely reflected God's good character— Adam as male and Eve as female. They were perfect reflections of God's Heart, in glorious fellowship with Him. God loved them, and He placed Adam in His beautiful garden to tend and to keep (Genesis 2:15). Adam and Eve trusted God there. They loved Him and had a good relationship with Him.

God gave Adam one command in the Garden of Eden. His command reflected true love between them, as their obedience to His command would demonstrate their reciprocated love for Him. True love in relationships is never forced. It is always derived from a choice that is made between two parties.

God, the Artist, Maker, and Creator, told Adam the truth in His command.

> And the Lord God commanded the man, saying, "You may surely eat of every tree of the garden, but of the tree of the knowledge of good and evil you shall not eat, for in the day that you eat of it you shall surely die" (Genesis 2:16–17).

Adam could trust God and obey Him, or distrust and disobey Him.

Adam and Eve were not totally alone in the Garden of Eden. The enemy of God's creation, Satan, appeared there as a serpent with evil intentions. God in His infinite wisdom allowed him to be there because He wanted to give Adam and Eve the choice to obey or disobey His command. By allowing Satan to be in the Garden of Eden, God was giving Adam and Eve the opportunity to choose to trust God wholeheartedly. He was providing them with the option to continue to love Him freely.

In the Garden of Eden, Satan tempted Eve into believing that God was withholding something from her when He commanded Adam and Eve to not eat from the Tree of the Knowledge of Good and Evil. Satan told Eve to eat from this tree. Even though God provided Eve with beautiful trees all around her, Satan lied to Eve about God's good character. He led her to doubt, distrust, and sin against God. After Eve took of the fruit from the Tree of the Knowledge of Good and Evil and ate it, she gave some to Adam (Genesis 3:1–4). By eating this fruit, Adam disobeyed God, and they both broke perfect fellowship with Him. This is where the separation between the Artist and His Art began. This is where the hearts of humankind turned away from God, and sin and death entered the world.

Today, Satan continues to attempt to ruin God's Art by stealing, killing, and destroying lives all over the world. He may not appear as a serpent, but he is actively deceiving God's creation in numerous ways. The Bible says that Satan prowls around like a roaring lion, seeking someone to devour (1 Peter 5:8). He is the angel of death and only desires to lie to and hurt God's creation. He is the author of confusion and the instigator of condemnation.

Because Adam and Eve sinned against God, all of humankind is born with a sinful nature. In our sinful nature, we are prone to sin in our hearts. Like Adam and Eve did, humankind falls for Satan's deceptive tactics and believes the father of lies. Our hearts go astray from our Creator. In them, we experience separation from God—doubt, shame, confusion, hate, fear, and more.

Though this is a tough truth to swallow, God is all-powerful. Like every artist making a beautiful masterpiece, God had a plan to redeem His Art. God foreknew that humankind would disobey Him. He foresaw what would happen in the Garden of Eden. He knew that Adam's sin would bring death into the world. As the ultimate Creator of life, the greatest Artist of all creation, He would become the Redeemer of all who would receive Him into their hearts. He would give them His life and bring them back into true fellowship with Him, whoever lives and is sovereign over all. He would rescue and protect them.

In Adam and Eve's and our rebellion against Him, God's love for humanity would remain constant. Adam and Eve broke fellowship with Him, but God was not going to leave us lost, shattered, and ashamed. Today, God does not want us to be eternally separated from Him. He does not want to leave us in darkness and enslaved to obeying the sinful desires in our hearts. This would only bring physical and spiritual death for our minds, bodies, and souls. God loves us and wants a different destiny for us. He wants to redeem and restore us in His steadfast love. He wants to give us the freedom to liberally obey and worship Him again.

God's plan to redeem His Art is found in Genesis 3:15 (NASB): "And I will put enmity Between you and the woman, And between your seed and her Seed; He shall bruise your head, And you shall bruise His heel." Here, God's Word triumphs. He proclaims the first prophecy of Jesus' coming to earth as a sinless and blameless man Who would ultimately defeat the powers of sin and death on the cross. He spoke directly to Satan about His coming and how He would eventually bruise his head. God, through His only begotten Son, Jesus Christ, would make the way for humanity to be reconciled to Him. God's motive? His unconditional love for us. "For God so loved the world, that he gave his only Son, that whoever believes in him should not perish but have eternal life" (John 3:16).

Before a holy and just God, our sinful actions lead to death. We cannot assume otherwise, as we are not our own lawgivers. God, our Creator, Maker, and Artist, made us, and we are accountable to Him. As sinners before Him, we are doomed to death. We are sentenced to eternal separation from our Artist.

"But God shows His love for us in that while we were still sinners, Christ died for us" (Romans 5:8). Even in our brokenness, in our depravity, in our rebellious, sinful nature, God's love draws us to a state of repentance from our sins.

In God's love, Jesus Christ died on the cross for our sinful actions past, present, and future. By His precious blood shed on the cross, Jesus Christ ransoms us from the hand and power of Satan (Ephesians 1:7). This is God's perfect, unconditional, agape love for you and for me. It is a constant, steadfast, and unchanging love that transcends time and space, into the dark and deadly hearts of men and women today. It lifts our lost and fallen souls out of horrible pits and raises us into new life in Christ. God's love for you reaches past the powers of sin and death. His love is so strong that it can heal lost, broken, and hurting hearts. It can give light to the captive heart. Romans 8:38–39 says, "For I am sure that neither death nor life, nor angels nor rulers, nor things present nor things to come, nor powers, nor height nor depth, nor anything else in all creation, will be able to separate us from the love of God in Christ Jesus our Lord."

In Jesus Christ, God's Art is redeemed. Because He is risen, our hearts are made alive again. In Him, our hearts can hear our Creator's voice, and we can leap for joy. In His presence, we can rest, for He is our true home base. We are renamed as God's children—forever loved and forgiven for eternity. We read His Word and are enlightened by His Holy Spirit. Unlike anything we have ever known, God's Word is faithful, pure, and true. His direction, guidance, and discipline become real to us, and we respond to Him.

In His creation, we look at the bright sun and fluffy clouds, and we see His incredible handiwork. Our hearts take notice of Him, and we rejoice in knowing our Creator. He gives us breath. He gives us faith. He gives us forgiveness. He is who we need. In Christ, there is fellowship. There is a relationship.

Rather than walk in darkness, we can walk in color.

There is an exchange between the Artist and His Art; communication between the two once again. In Jesus Christ, we are reunited with our original Artist.

Unlike Adam and Eve, and their sinful descendants (us), Jesus Christ was and is a perfect Man. He is morally pure. In the Bible, Jesus is called the Second Adam. He is the image of the invisible God, the firstborn of all creation (Colossians 1:15). He is the reflection of God's amazing love, displayed for all to see. While he was here on earth, He trusted His Father and obeyed His will perfectly. "And being found in human form, He humbled himself by becoming obedient to the point of death, even death on a cross" (Philippians 2:8). God's everlasting love was demonstrated on the cross, where He poured Himself out for us. Jesus Christ gave Himself for a rebellious people, with hearts that sinned against God. Jesus is the Son of God and did what we as fallen creatures could never do before God's eyes. Christ's death on the cross fulfilled God's perfect will (Hebrews 10:7). Because of Who Jesus is and what He has done on the cross, we can be accepted in Him, in the Beloved—in God's sight. Jesus' blood shed on the cross is a sufficient and just payment for the sins of humanity.

"Behold, My servant will prosper, He will be high and lifted up and greatly exalted. Just as many were astonished at you, My people, So His appearance was marred more than any man And His form more than the sons of men" (Isaiah 52:13–14 NASB).

"All of us like sheep have gone astray, Each of us has turned to his own way; But the Lord has caused the iniquity of us all To fall on Him" (Isaiah 53:6 NASB).

"He shall see the labor of His soul, and be satisfied. By His knowledge My righteous Servant shall justify many, For He shall bear their iniquities" (Isaiah 53:11 NKJV).

Unlike fallen humankind's, the heart and mind of Christ are pure (Proverbs 30:5). He is eternal, holy, and righteous (Isaiah 6:3–4). He is the true beauty of God's tapestry. He is good and went about doing good while He was on earth. Jesus is wonderful to gaze upon and cherish for all of eternity. He gives humanity spiritual life, light, and peace that surpass all understanding (Philippians 4:7). He gives the guilty mercy and the brokenhearted comfort. He offers forgiveness to the sinner and accepts the flawed. To those who are confused, He is the Way, the Truth, and the Life. No one comes to the Father except through Him (John 14:6). Full of grace and truth, Jesus Christ is Who we all need, all the time. Because of Who He is and what He has done for us on the cross, we can have hope in His eternal redemption for us.

So we now see.

Jesus is the One Who can set us free—free to become who God made us to be.

Receiving the Artist's Invitation

> The true Christian life, when we live near to God, is the rough draft of the life of full communion above. We have seen the artist make with his pencil, or with his charcoal, a bare outline of his picture. It is nothing more, but still one could guess what the finished picture will be from the sketch before you. One acquainted with the artist could see upon the canvas all the splendor of color peeping through the dark lines of the pencil.
>
> —*Sermons of Rev. C. H. Spurgeon of London* (1884)

Since I was a little girl, I loved to blend colors with different art mediums and sketch God's beautiful creation—birds, trees, and flowers. At home in my spare time, I enjoyed using my imagination to write stories. Words allowed a quiet kid like me to freely express strong emotions, thoughts, and feelings. Chapter books kept me up at night; I used to sneak my flashlight under my covers to read in the dark. I didn't care if I got caught reading after my bedtime. I was captivated by another world, one I didn't know existed yet. I didn't know the way to get there, though. So I lost myself in these pages that spoke of make-believe places.

At the age of twenty-seven, I finally placed my faith in Jesus Christ. When I came to Him, I was a mess. I was deeply involved in a sinful life—enslaved in my mind and heart to a false doctrine called the New Age movement.[5] Right away, though, when I came to Jesus, He miraculously healed my mind, body, and soul. His blood covered me and cleansed me from wicked works. At the cross, I became His forgiven and free creature. Immediately after God revealed Himself

---

5 https://www.gotquestions.org/new-age-movement.html

to me, I realized I was a slave to sin. Now, I had a choice to worship God. Heavy chains were holding me down in my own prison, but Jesus released me from them. God allowed me to recognize that I had a choice to respond to His love for me.

Shortly after Jesus rescued me, I decided to study God's Word.

My soul longed to know her own true Artist.

Now that Jesus Christ was in my life, I was certain that this foreign place I sought out as a little girl was no longer make-believe. I knew heaven was real. I could feel God's presence in me. His story was true. With my eyes opened, I could read it, in my heart. Psalm 119:105 says, "Your word is a lamp to my feet and a light to my path." So I chose to set my heart on pilgrimage, to this Promised Land (Psalm 84:5).

Once my Creator found my soul and touched its depths, I knew there was no one else in the world who knew me like He did. He was the One Who formed me in my mother's womb (Psalm 139:13). He was the Prince I needed to be rescued by; my One true love. He was and is the God-Man Who died for me. My hero. Only He could meet my deepest needs. We belonged together, for eternity. I wanted to work out my salvation, so I could be with Him and praise Him forever.

Deeper than the longing to develop any artistic skills, I yearned to intimately commune with the One Who made me.

I believe He knew this, and I'm grateful for His plan to redeem me, His creation.

God, I learned, is an incredible Artist.

His love drew me to Himself.

He draws on our hearts, writes on them, and turns them towards His Heart, where we belong, in Him.

So when God gave me this quote by C. H. Spurgeon in the early years of my journey with Him, I trusted that He had a good plan for me. Even after I placed my faith in Jesus Christ, I was still a total mess inside my heart. It didn't matter, though. Who I was did not determine Who He is and what He could do inside of me. He was the One Who was making something beautiful out of the mess I was giving Him. He was the One drawing, creating, and cleansing me as He saw fit, for His glory.

His invitation to trust Him as my Artist was handed to me, and I said "Yes."

Will you?

My Creator

I'm captivated by Your story.
You're the Author of life, breathing words into existence before You.
You said, "Let there be light" and there was
light. You make us brand new.

I'm drawn to your sovereignty.
Writing and entering your own script, You
became flesh and dwelt among us.
You tell us, "I am the Resurrection and the
Life." You gave up your rights.

I'm in awe of Your humility.
You're the Redeemer of humanity, filling empty
spaces in the most unlikely places.
You say to the thief, "I will see you in paradise."
You paid the ultimate price.

I'm enthralled by Your vision.
You're the Artist of all creation, painting multi-
dimensional skies and souls of men that arise.
You say, "I am coming quickly." You will come for Your Bride.

I'm in love with Your Heart.
You're the Lover of sinners, extending wedding
invitations to the poor and the lame on highways.
You call, "Come to me." We respond to
Your voice and follow Your ways.

You are JESUS.
You are HE.
You are ours forever, for all of eternity.

 **Application**

Fellowship with our Creator was broken through a lack of trust in Him. Before she ever ate the fruit from the Tree of the Knowledge of Good and Evil, Eve and God were in a perfect relationship with each other. Adam also was in glorious communion with His Maker.

It was Eve's pride that got in the way of her relationship with God. It was Adam's disobedience that led to humankind's fall. They sinned against Him. Their faith in God was torn apart by disbelief in His Word.

In God's perfect timing, the Word became flesh and dwelt among us (John 1:14). Jesus Christ entered this dark and sinful world to humbly die on the cross for us sinners. For the separated to become reunited with God, Jesus Christ lived the perfect life we could never live, died for us, and resurrected from the grave so that we could have eternal life in Him.

This is beautiful. This is truth. This is love. This is grace.

Jesus Christ is the light of the world.

He gives us new life, in color, in Him.

Though we all deserve death for the sins we've committed in our lives, God wants to give us eternal life in His only begotten Son, Jesus Christ.

When we trust in Jesus Christ as our Lord and Savior, we become new creations in Him (2 Corinthians 5:17). We become God's heartwork, whom He is redeeming and restoring for His glory and honor.

How does this happen? God's Holy Spirit comes to dwell inside of believers—in our hearts. The Holy Spirit inside of us gives us a new desire to seek the things of God. Through this supernatural work of God, our souls are revived. Our spiritual eyes are opened to notice God's presence. Our spiritual ears are healed to hear God's voice through His Word, by His Holy Spirit. Our hearts are pointed to the One Who loves us unreservedly. We are reunited with God, our original Artist, the One Who knit us together in our mother's womb (Psalm 139:13). We are no longer separated from our Creator. We know our Maker, and our Maker knows us.

Perhaps, you are deciding for the first time that you want to receive Jesus Christ as your personal Lord and Savior. You've lived your life your own way, and all this has produced is death. You are done living a life of emptiness. You've heard about Jesus and what He has done for you on the cross, and you are ready to give Him your heart. You would like to place your heart back into your Artist's hands to do as He pleases.

I encourage you to say a prayer in your heart like this, in your own words:

> God in heaven, I stand before You guilty for my sins. You see who I really am—a sinner in desperate need of a Savior. Please forgive me for all of my sins, God. I'm done living life my own way. I believe You sent Jesus Christ into the world to walk the earth as a sinless man, live a perfect life, and die on the cross for my sins. I believe in my heart that He rose from the dead and is now seated at Your right hand. Thank You for Your perfect love, God. Wash and cleanse me with the blood of the Lamb. Please send Your Holy Spirit to dwell in me. Give me a hunger and thirst for Your Word, and help me to learn to walk in Your ways. Mold and shape my heart into who You created me to be and use me for Your glory and honor. In Jesus' name. Amen.

Genesis 1:31: What did God make? How do we know it was very good?

_____
_____
_____
_____
_____
_____
_____
_____

Genesis 3:1–15: How did the serpent lie to Eve? What was the result of Eve believing in his lie?

_____
_____
_____
_____
_____
_____
_____
_____

Romans 5:8: How did God show sinners His love? What does His love provide for sinners?

_____
_____
_____
_____
_____
_____
_____

Giving Your Heart Perspective

Prior to sketching an image, an artist should have a reference point. This point should determine the angles as well as the height, width, and depth of the image. From the reference point, artists can sketch an idea of the image they have in their minds. If there is no reference point for their artwork, the sketched image will look indefinite, imbalanced, and unspecified. The absence of a reference point breeds the lack of a foundation for their final creation.

As noted in the book, *Walking in Victory*, by Dennis McCallum, "Meaning and value are either determined by referring to God, our infinite, external reference point, or they are manufactured and changed at will by the shifting relative evaluations of the individual or the crowd" (p. 35). Here, we see the importance of referring to God as our reference point. He is where we find meaning, value, identity, and so on. As an artist identifies his reference point before he sketches an image, so God has shown us that He Himself is our infinite, external reference point. In Him, we are found and known by our Creator.

John 1:1–4 says, "In the beginning was the Word, and the Word was with God, and the Word was God. He was in the beginning with God. All things were made through him, and without him was not any thing made that was made. In Him was life, and the life was the light of men." Genesis 1:1 says, "In the beginning, God created the heavens and the earth." "For by him all things were created, in heaven and on earth, visible and invisible, whether thrones or dominions or rulers or authorities—all things were created through him and for him" (Colossians 1:16).

Jesus Christ is the only begotten Son of God. He is the Word became flesh Who dwelt among us. He is the Almighty I AM. He is self-existent and sovereign over all of creation.

Jesus shares seven "I AM" statements in the Gospel of John alone.

First, Jesus said, "I am the bread of life. He who comes to Me shall never hunger" (John 6:35).

Second, Jesus said, "I am the light of the world" (John 8:12).

Third, Jesus said, "I am the door" (John 10:9).

Fourth, Jesus said, "I am the true vine" (John 15:1).

Fifth, Jesus said, "I am the good shepherd. The good shepherd gives His life for the sheep" (John 10:11).

Sixth, Jesus said in John 11:25, "I am the resurrection and the life."

Seventh, Jesus said, "I am the way, the truth, and the life. No one comes to the Father except through Me" (John 14:6).[6]

Jesus Christ is Who we need. He is our Foundation, our Rock, and our Salvation. We are complete in Him (Colossians 2:9–10).

God, as He has proclaimed, is the moral, spiritual, and physical lawgiver of the universe. Regardless of whether we acknowledge Him

---

[6] https://billygraham.org/decision-magazine/february-2008/the-i-ams-of-jesus/

or live by our own relative beliefs, He is Who He says He is, and He is in control. All of creation is dependent upon Him.

Without our true reference point, though, our hearts have no perspective. Without Jesus Christ, our hearts are lost, leading us in directions we only *think* are true.

When we look around the world today, we hear about the notion of relativism. According to *The Stanford Encyclopedia of Philosophy*, "relativism, roughly put, is the view that truth and falsity, right and wrong, standards of reasoning, and procedures of justification are products of differing conventions and frameworks of assessment and that their authority is confined to the context giving rise to them."[7] In this mindset, there is no personal reference point. People are left to believe in what they assume is true, what they want to believe is true. The idea of relativism encourages people to make up their own reference point.

There is a movement today that embraces all belief systems. It is called the New Age movement,[8] what Jesus delivered me from when I initially came to Him. It encourages men and women to make up their own belief system and tolerate what does not align with their reality, what they would like to believe is true. This movement promotes the idea that we can all believe in what we want to believe in and embrace each other's way of life. It dictates that the Hindu can exist with the Christian, and the Christian can exist with the Buddhist.

The New Age movement looks to humankind to redeem the world, rather than Jesus Christ, the only begotten Son of God. It highlights that we can save ourselves through the alteration of our thoughts and actions. Through this doctrine, people are taught to perform rituals and practices such as yoga, meditation, and positive "I am"

---

[7] https://plato.stanford.edu/entries/relativism/
[8] https://www.gotquestions.org/new-age-movement.html

affirmations to raise their level of consciousness, which would lead them into a new way of thinking and living. It falsely promotes a better life and world for humanity. Under this mindset, people offer only a guise of peace and righteousness.

In human eyes, the New Age movement looks appealing, as everyone desires to do what they want to do and achieve world peace. It sounds very good. Nearly everyone in the world wants a better outcome, place, and ending for humanity. They also want to live their own way. This movement seems to support this endeavor and work towards harmony for all people, regardless of their background. It gathers together different men and women from various religions and deludes them into thinking they can overcome darkness as one humanity.

But appearance is not everything. Appearances can be deceiving.

"For the Lord sees not as man sees: man looks on the outward appearance, but the Lord looks on the heart" (1 Samuel 16:7). God can see what is in our heart. He can see past falsehood; the Bible says, "the heart is deceitful above all things, and desperately sick; who can understand it?" (Jeremiah 17:9). Our hearts, left unchecked by the Word of God, lead us away from our true reference point.

When Adam and Eve sinned against Him, God knew where they were in the Garden of Eden and what they did. Though they tried to hide behind fig leaves after they rebelled, God could see everything in Adam and Eve. They disobeyed God's Word, and they were ashamed. This is why they hid from God. They attempted to cover up their sin with fig leaves. But God knew what they did.

God's Word never changes, even throughout the generations that have passed since He made Adam and Eve. God knows the depths of deception behind the New Age movement, as it reflects the depths of deception in the human heart. This movement, this doctrine has no real foundation. It is rooted in lies that are misleading many hearts away from their true reference point. Without relying on the Word of God as our standard, we are caught up in a lifestyle that appeals to our sinful desires.

Put simply, Hinduism cannot coexist with Christianity, nor can Buddhism align with Christianity when God's Word says there is only one way to God (John 14:6). "Jesus said to him, 'I am the way, and the truth, and the life. No one comes to the Father except through me'" (John 14:6). God is the Ultimate Artist, and He Himself is our reference point. His thoughts are not our thoughts, and our ways are not His ways. "'For my thoughts are not your thoughts, neither are your ways my ways,' declares the Lord. 'For as the heavens are higher than the earth, so are my ways higher than your ways and my thoughts than your thoughts'" (Isaiah 55:8–9). While the New Age movement spreads the notion that all paths lead to God, God's Word says salvation is in no one else but Jesus Christ (Acts 4:12).

The truth is, as Satan appeared before Adam and Eve in the Garden of Eden, so Satan disguises himself as an angel of light in our world through the New Age movement today. "And no wonder, for even Satan disguises himself as an angel of light" (2 Corinthians 11:14). In the Garden of Eden, Satan lied to Eve in the form of a serpent as he lies to humanity in the form of this beautiful-looking doctrine today. The serpent was cunning in the Garden of Eden, and Satan remains crafty in luring others to this false doctrine. He looked harmless in the Garden of Eden, as this movement looks harmless.

Yet, God's Word prevails.

God is light, and in Him is no darkness at all (1 John 1:5). He exposes darkness and shows us that the New Age movement is rooted in lies. The spiritual power behind this belief that all paths lead to God derives from Satan himself. The offer to create one's own reality or be like God is enticing to our sinful nature. If we fall for this lie, though, we are essentially falling for the same lie Eve believed in the

Garden of Eden: "For God knows that when you eat of it your eyes will be opened, and you will be like God, knowing good and evil" (Genesis 3:5). In her heart, Eve became proud. She left her reference point and settled for a lie that only left her indefinite, imbalanced, and unspecified. When Eve broke fellowship with her Maker, she no longer had a foundation, a perspective. She was outside of God's will. In sin, she became lost, confused, and ashamed.

Humankind's fall and this movement started with doubt in the heart of man. It began with believing lies similar to Satan's original lies told in the Garden of Eden.

In Genesis 3:1–5, we read, "Now the serpent was more crafty than any other beast of the field that the Lord God had made. He said to the woman, 'Did God actually say, "You shall not eat of any tree in the Garden"?' And the woman said to the serpent, 'We may eat of the fruit of the trees in the garden, but God said, "You shall not eat of the fruit of the tree that is in the midst of the garden, neither shall you touch it, lest you die."' But the serpent said to the woman, 'You will not surely die. For God knows that when you eat of it your eyes will be opened, and you will be like God, knowing good and evil.'"

As part of the New Age movement, people engage in yoga, meditation, and positive affirmation practices, endorsing the idea that human beings can be like God. Yoga and meditation are rooted in Hinduism and Buddhism, religions that reflect that people can be their own gods. God sees these attempts to be like Him, and He sees them as filthy rags. Although these practices appear harmless, they are deceiving. Man's heart can be led astray by them and fall into the broad road of destruction (Matthew 7:13). The consequence of going down this path is hell.

Isaiah 14:12–15 says, "How you are fallen from heaven, O Day Star, son of Dawn! How you are cut down to the ground, you who laid the nations low! You said in your heart, 'I will ascend to heaven; above the stars of God I will set my throne on high; I will sit on the mount of assembly in the far reaches of the north; I will ascend above the heights of the clouds; I will make myself like the Most High.' But you are brought down to Sheol, to the far reaches of the pit." Pride brought Satan low when he initially rebelled against God. Pride brings us low, as we try to be our own god.

It is important to note that the current world education system is promoting many of these ideals of relativism and the New Age movement. Through these ideals, Satan is luring men and women to stray from God and His original intent for them. Psalm 51:6 says, "Behold, you delight in truth in the inward being, and you teach me wisdom in the secret heart." If humankind does not perceive reality through the lens of God's Word, they will remain in a state of ignorance. They will become like the world and reflect deception, not what God initially designed for them. Ignorance can only lead our minds and hearts to destruction. Without the law, the life, and the light of the world, we will roam this earth devoid of purpose. We will be empty and vain, out of order and in chaos. We will make decisions that seem right to us but only lead to death (Proverbs 14:12).

There are other examples of humankind straying from God and His original intent for them: same-sex marriages, human trafficking, and drug use. Today, people are instilling ideas of tolerance for sin into uninformed minds and hearts. There are books, music videos, and TV shows that advertise the appeal of these lifestyles. Though they appeal to our sinful and rebellious human nature, they are deceptive traps of Satan for the soul. A heart with no true reference point easily falls for these paths and needs to be rescued from the powers of sin and darkness in their lives.

Looking to the Artist

I grew up in an average suburban area in Southern California. I recall my parents taking me to a Catholic church for a period of time. By standing in the pews, I learned a few songs that remained in my heart throughout the years. One of them, "You Are Mine," consistently popped into my mind as I charted unknown territory later in life. More specifically, when I was on the broad road (Matthew 7:13).

> Do not be afraid, I am with you
> I have called you each by name
> Come and follow Me
> I will bring you home
> I love you and you are mine.[9]

I don't remember hearing the Word of God in church or at home.

By the time I was five years old, my mom and dad divorced. The home my sisters and I once found comfort in became a broken place. After the divorce, our family was quickly torn apart. My mom, sisters, and I moved out of our house and into a small apartment (the first of many). My dad also moved out and into a small apartment, until he bought a new house. He eventually remarried a woman named Grace, and she had three daughters. They had one child together; they also began to foster children and eventually adopted one. My mom carried her own burdens after the divorce, as she struggled to provide for her three daughters. Later on, she got into a relationship but did not choose to remarry.

In my early childhood, I experienced ongoing depression and physical ailments that I believe were a natural response to the disruptions in

---

[9] Peter De Angelis and Robert P. Marcucci, "You Are Mine." Universal Music Publishing Group.

my life that I had not yet fully processed. My innocence was tainted at the age of five, and this became an ongoing nuisance in my heart and mind. I could hide it from others, but I could never run away from it myself. At the age of eight, I was in and out of the hospital because of stomach issues. I also attended speech therapy for years. Aside from the divorce, the unsettling circumstances in my life caused me to hide my thoughts and feelings from people—parents, counselors, and even friends.

In school, I tried my best to put my entire past behind me and excel in the world by earning good grades and being involved in healthy extracurricular activities. I got involved in clubs and activities, like Dance/Drill Team. I was on student government and volunteered in the community. I had a great circle of friends and was often viewed as the "go-to" girl if people had problems in their lives. I was a goal setter and achiever, determined to live differently than my present reality.

As a preteen, I returned to the Catholic Church. A friend from school invited me. Going to church seemed like a good thing for me to do, so I pursued it. During this season, my view of God developed. After volunteering as an usher and sitting in a pew during Mass on a weekly basis, I began to see Him as a big God whose expectations I could never meet. *Could He ever understand me?* In my heart, I began to grow bored of religion. I started to fall asleep while the priest talked. But I continued to go through the motions of going to church because I wanted approval from God and others.

One day, I confessed my sins to a priest. I didn't tell him what I really felt ashamed of though. After listening to my verbal confession and discovering that I was only eleven years old and hadn't completed my sacraments yet, the priest scolded me. He told me I was not allowed to confess my sins to him because I had not made my First Holy Communion yet. I didn't know how to react to him. So I ran out of the confession stand with a red face, full of shame and embarrassment. Sitting in the pews with my face buried in my hands, I wept. After this happened, I was determined to make my Holy Communion with the Catholic Church and be made right with God.

A couple of years later, I did. But I still felt empty inside.

During and after college, I traveled, volunteered, and studied in many different places around the world, including Cuba, El Salvador, Italy, and Washington DC. Culture, diversity, and coloring outside of the lines became more and more interesting to me. In these experiences, I felt like I could explore and discover who I was apart from my family and Catholic background. In all of these experiences, I sought for more—something deeper than what I knew to be true at the time.

After earning my master's degree and working for a nonprofit in New York City, I thought I would be satisfied (or at least content), like every other normal twentysomething. In this role, I was making a difference and helping people in many different capacities.

But I still felt empty inside my heart. I felt dead. This discontentment continued for another five years.

In my mid-twenties, I began to rebel and wholeheartedly search for the truth. I started to drink and let loose in bars and places where I could talk, think, and dance however I wanted. Over time, I began to believe in many empty philosophies, like the notion of relativism. But even this wasn't enough for me.

After a while, I became so fed up with the world and curious about the meaning of life that I sought healing for my mind, body, and soul in the New Age movement. Thinking that I simply needed to make some changes in my life, I joined a life coaching program, and over a period of a few months, I became brainwashed by self-help philosophies. After adopting this New Age mindset, I began to practice its principles in my mind and heart.

Like Eve, I became proud through the New Age movement. It looked appealing, innocent, and almost right. It appeared harmless and even used words like "God," "love," and "light" in its teachings.

I had searched for the truth in so many other places. This seemed like the right fit for me. *Finally*, I thought. *I discovered the secret to living a life of fulfillment.*

While following this lifestyle, I started to experience my dream in every area of my life. It felt good. One of my dreams was to visit schools that promoted these spiritual principles and creativity. I wanted to help children become whole, not just in their minds, but in their hearts and souls as well. I also met the man I thought was my soul mate. We shared similar backgrounds and were headed in a similar direction for our lives. As I surrounded myself with like-minded people, I was assured that everyone could simply create their own love filled reality.

After I returned to New York City from my trip across the United States, I cohosted a three-day conference for children that focused on creativity and mindfulness. I figured we could all raise their level of consciousness and promote good in the world.

This lie only led me down the broad road of destruction.

Soon enough, my dream became a nightmare.

The man I thought was my soul mate at this time suddenly died. While accomplishing his dream on a trip to Brazil, he fell on a rock in the Tijuca forest and lost all consciousness. Although two other men were with him, they did not help him, and he died.

Six months later, I nearly died.

Though this lifestyle felt wonderful for some time, sin eventually caught up with us. This false appearance of light showed its true colors.

It was satanic.

It was not light at all. It was dark.

Today, I see how Satan uses this lie to lead many souls to hell.

For six months, I tried to heal from my loved one's passing, but one day, I finally broke down. There was something very real in me that made it clear that I needed help outside of myself.

When I became fed up with the misery, confusion, and emptiness deep inside of my heart, I cried out for help. With every part of my being, I screamed at the top of my lungs to the living God. The words that formed and uttered from my lips were, "Use me!!" My body leaned against a wall as I surrendered and cried out for someone to rescue me. I yelled as loud as possible. Deep in my heart, I believed that if there were a God, He could really hear me. He could hear my desperate cry.

A couple of days later, I entered a behavioral health center and psychiatric hospital. Through a series of events, God allowed me to recognize that I was captive, under the power of the enemy of my soul, Satan.

In the psychiatric hospital, my dad and his wife, Grace, who recently became believers in Jesus Christ, came to visit me. My mom and her boyfriend, Albert, also came to visit me.

Surrounded by four white walls and other patients in the hospital, I begged God for His mercy. Although I didn't know Him personally yet, I believed that He was now in control. I started to see that He was real, and He was revealing Himself to me.

I needed Him.

Grace, my stepmom, gently told me that I didn't need to reveal my heart to God (like I thought I did). I didn't need to do any of the things I was practicing in the New Age movement. God already knew my heart. God is all knowing.

This truth opened up my eyes to the reality that I had been deceived in this New Age lifestyle.

Over the next few days, the Holy Spirit showed me that Satan comes to kill, steal, and destroy. Jesus has come so that we might have abundant life in Him (John 10:10).

I was on the broad road of destruction. Jesus came to rescue me from this path.

Through the adoption of this New Age mindset, Satan filled my mind and heart with lies. This lifestyle leads souls to hell; it is dangerous.

After so many days in the hospital, my true Advocate, Jesus Christ, and Judge, God, showed me mercy. I was released from the hospital without any court-ordered treatment. The counselor's only request was for me to go home with my family to California.

Like a prodigal returning home to her heavenly father, I moved in with my dad and recognized that I needed a Savior.

There, I heard the Gospel with an open heart and gave my life to Jesus Christ.

> For God so loved the world, that he gave his only Son,
> that whoever believes in him should not perish but
> have eternal life (John 3:16).

By God's love and grace, I was miraculously rescued, delivered, and healed in my mind, heart, soul, and body.

God did what I could never do: He loved me, and He showed me the cross.

Jesus Christ, God in the flesh, is the God-Man Who died for me.

He loved me at my darkest.

After Jesus saved me from this deceptive New Age lifestyle, three more acquaintances I knew who practiced this way of life abruptly passed away. These events all happened around the same time, one after another. The ultimate ending for their lives broke my heart. I am sure it broke God's Heart too. His Heart of love grieves when a soul is misled, off the grid of what His plan was for them.

I learned through these experiences that God is a God of truth. Regardless of whether mankind believes in the truth, the truth never changes. His love never changes. "The sum of your word is truth, and every one of your righteous rules endures forever" (Psalm 119:160). Matthew 7:13–14 says, "Enter by the narrow gate. For the gate is wide and the way is easy that leads to destruction, and those who enter by it are many. For the gate is narrow and the way is hard that leads to life, and those who find it are few." God desires that all people be saved and to come to the knowledge of the truth (1 Timothy 2:4).

Jesus Christ is our only true reference point.

In the New Age movement, my heart had no true reference point. Because my heart had no perspective, it fell for the deceptive tactics of the enemy.

It was a proud heart, a lost heart, a deceived heart.

A hurting heart, a broken heart, and an empty heart.

A sinful heart.

What my heart truly needed was a Savior, God's love. Jesus Christ. As a broken girl from a broken home, I looked for love in all the wrong places. I ached for wholeness. I was desperate for peace. I wanted harmony. But everything I attempted to use to satisfy my soul was false. These wrong places seemed good for some time. But they eventually fell short of the only true resting place for my heart—Jesus Christ.

You might be able to relate.

I looked for love at home.

I looked for love at school by earning good grades, degrees, and certificates.

I looked for love in religion, through Catholicism, a New Age lifestyle, and even church.

I looked for love in men.

I looked for love in friends.

I looked for love in partying.

I even looked for love in strangers.

It wasn't until God allowed me to reach the end of myself, in the darkest prison of my soul, that I finally reached out to Him.

The Almighty I AM.

When I saw who I was and what I did before my Creator, I knew I deserved hell. But then He showed me true love.

Jesus Christ.

God, the Father, chose to love me through His only begotten Son, Jesus Christ.

Jesus Christ came down from heaven by the power of the Holy Spirit and became a man to walk the earth in perfect obedience to the Father. He died for my sins on the cross, and He rose from the dead. Because He is my Lord and Savior, Jesus Christ delivered my soul from death and my feet from stumbling so that I may walk before Him in the land of the living (Psalm 116:8–9).

I was undeserving and wretched, a sinner to my core, but somehow, God loved me perfectly, the one He made for Himself. He didn't love me for any reason. He didn't look at my outer appearance. He loved me unconditionally.

God's love for me was out of this world. It was heavenly and pure.

So when I finally looked to my Artist, His unconditional love flooded my soul. His life came into my heart. His light shone on my darkness.

From that day forward, I looked to Him as my reference point in every aspect of my journey. Even when I didn't feel Him or see Him at work, I knew He was with me because He is the Almighty I AM.

He is the One we look to for meaning, value, and identity.

Love incarnate, we are whole and complete in Christ (Colossians 2:10).

Perhaps you are seeking direction in your life. Or you might be looking for love, like I did in the world. You might be a wanderer like I was, exploring and accepting all kinds of different beliefs. You need a reference point, though, the truth to guide you. Even if you never grew up with the knowledge of God or you've walked away from your faith in Jesus Christ, you can still choose to look to Him today.

Will you?

He is a sure foundation for all who are lost and in need of salvation.

Close

In despair, I searched for my Neverland; my Emerald City.
Though I felt pain and misery, I knew there had
to be a place of refuge and tranquility.
They told me to find it in a man, a career, and even a house
but I said, "No, this place is close, as close as my heart."
So, I sought and I sought, flyin' and roamin' around,
here, there and everywhere from dawn until dark.

Like Eve, like Paul, like the child who lost it all, I fell for
the old Serpent's lies, and slept with the enemy.
Too foolish to see, too vain to concede, I wandered with the
Angel of Light and embraced his façade in all his beauty.
They told me to keep makin' magic, keep livin' my dream, so
I did and alleged, "Yes, this place is real, as real as can be."
So, I sought and sought in his lavish playground,
'til the god of this world blinded me.

In confusion, I wept for my Neverland; my Emerald
City, "Oh, isn't it close? As real as can be?"
White walls all around me, nurses tried to tame
me, *You* opened my eyes to the adversary:
Perverted bliss. Rubber gum. Fake mist in a palace
slum, I couldn't believe he deceived me.

A battle like I've never seen, Your Angel Armies came to intervene;
they fought and fought 'til my heart surrendered to Thee.
My God, my Savior, I cried at Your feet, "How could you
ever take me? Your Grace and Mercy are too vast for me."

Like David, like Jonah, like Mary Magdalene in her mess, You
delivered my soul, and ransomed me from the Prince of darkness.
Undeserving and wretched, You told me I'm Yours, clothed
me in white and walked me through Your corridors.
A marvel too bright, an esteem too deep; by Your
cross, I'm forgiven, by your Love, I'm freed.

My Neverland; my Emerald City. You were close the whole time.
In despair, in misery, in confusion, You wanted me.
Only a whisper away, I couldn't see.
My sin obscured Your divinity.

To live and move and have my being in You, You
tore down the veil and ripped it in two.
No longer a captive in slavery, no longer a mystery,
The Way for us to be one was made known.
My Hero, My God, my Savior, Jesus Christ.
You set eternity in my heart from the beginning and
only You, only You could bring me Home.

Application

If you have lived your life wandering around the world in search of the truth, I encourage you to believe what God says in His Word. Jesus is the Almighty I AM. Through Him, God gives our hearts perspective.

Review Jesus' seven "I AM" statements.

"I am the bread of life. He who comes to Me shall never hunger" (John 6:35).

"I am the light of the world" (John 8:12).

"I am the door" (John 10:9).

"I am the true vine" (John 15:1).

"I am the good shepherd. The good shepherd gives His life for the sheep" (John 10:11).

"I am the resurrection and the life" (John 11:25).

"I am the way, the truth, and the life. No one comes to the Father except through Me" (John 14:6).[10]

If you haven't done so yet, open the Bible. The Bible is the Word of God. Through His Word, God gives you light. "The unfolding of your words gives light; it imparts understanding to the simple" (Psalm 119:130). "For the word of God is living and active, sharper than any two-edged sword, piercing to the division of soul and of spirit, of

---

[10] https://billygraham.org/decision-magazine/february-2008/the-i-ams-of-jesus/

joints and of marrow, and discerning the thoughts and intentions of the heart" (Hebrews 4:12).

My prayer for you is that God will enlighten the eyes of your heart. Let Him give you perspective. Allow the Holy Spirit to reveal all truth to you, even if it is different from what you've grown up with or believed up until now. John 8:32 says, "And you will know the truth, and the truth will set you free."

There is no other way, truth, or life we can find on earth; the only hope for our eternal souls is in Jesus Christ. When we're lost or confused, He is our reference point—the Almighty I AM. Knowing what He's done for us on the cross, we can come to Jesus exactly as we are and receive His work of salvation for us.

When Jesus was on the cross, He cried out, "It is finished!" John 19:30 says, "When Jesus had received the sour wine, he said, 'It is finished,' and he bowed his head and gave up his spirit." What was finished? God's work—Jesus Christ, the Son of God, came to do what the Father told Him to do while on earth. God's plan of redemption for humanity was accomplished through His Son, Jesus Christ, Who was and is and is to come. "He was foreknown before the foundation of the world but was made manifest in the last times for the sake of you who through him are believers in God, who raised him from the dead and gave him glory, so that your faith and hope are in God" (1 Peter 1:20–21). May God bring our hearts to a place of trust and hope in Him.

John 14:6: What is the way to God? How can we have a relationship with God?

_____
_____
_____
_____
_____
_____
_____
_____

John 11:25: What is life? How can we have eternal life?

_____
_____
_____
_____
_____
_____
_____
_____

Colossians 1:16: Who created everything? For whom were these things created?

_____
_____
_____
_____
_____
_____
_____

Sketching His Blueprint on Your Heart

Sketching is a skill. A sketch is a rough draft of the image in the artist's mind. It is what is written on paper before the final image is revealed. The Bible says that the law and the prophets in the Old Testament were only a shadow of the things that were to come; the reality, however, is found in Christ (Colossians 2:17; Hebrews 10:1). Essentially, the Old Testament in the Bible is a rough draft and foreshadowing of the coming of Jesus Christ. Jesus Christ is the exact image of the invisible God (Colossians 1:15).

In Matthew 5:17, Jesus says, "Do not think that I have come to abolish the Law or the Prophets; I have not come to abolish them but to fulfill them." Jesus is the fulfillment of the law and the prophets. "For the whole law is fulfilled in one word: 'You shall love your neighbor as yourself'" (Galatians 5:14). Love does no wrong to a neighbor; therefore love is the fulfilling of the law (Romans 13:10). That is Jesus, and His life, death, and resurrection revealed Who He is: love, the fulfillment of the law. He lived a perfect life, He died an undeserving death, and He rose from the dead by the power of the Holy Spirit. He is alive and is seated at the right hand of God (Mark 16:19).

We are guilty of breaking the perfect law of God. "For whoever keeps the whole law but fails in one point has become guilty of all of it" (James 2:10). "For out of the heart come evil thoughts, murder, adultery, sexual immorality, theft, false witness, slander" (Matthew 15:19). Jeremiah 17:9 says, "The heart is deceitful above all things, and desperately sick; who can understand it?" Without Jesus Christ, we are morally corrupt and deprived. We have a sinful nature. We fall short of the glory of God (Romans 3:23).

When we sin, our hearts condemn us. When we come to terms with the reality of our sin before a Holy God, we are horrified. Our hearts know we deserve hell.

But did you know that God is greater than our hearts (1 John 3:20)?

"But God demonstrates His own love toward us, in that while we were yet sinners, Christ died for us" (Romans 5:8). Jesus was the perfect sacrifice made on the cross for us; He shed His precious blood for us as a payment for our sin. God accepted His offering, His payment for our sin. "For Christ did not enter a holy place made with hands, a mere copy of the true one, but into heaven itself, now to appear in the presence of God for us" (Hebrews 9:24).

For who? For humanity, for the hearts of men and women.

When people receive Jesus Christ as their Lord and Savior, they become new creations in Christ (2 Corinthians 5:17). God forgives them for their sin. He gives them His Holy Spirit and writes His law upon their minds and hearts (Hebrews 8:10). This is why we are encouraged to read the Word of God on a daily basis. Romans 12:2 says, "Do not be conformed to this world, but be transformed by the renewal of your mind, that by testing you may discern what is the will of God, what is good and acceptable and perfect." Through this process, we are "renewed in knowledge according to the image of Christ, Who created him, where there is neither Greek nor Jew, circumcised nor uncircumcised, barbarian, Scythian, slave nor free, but Christ is all, and in all" (Colossians 3:10–11). God sketches His blueprint on our hearts, and we are made alive in our Lord and Savior, Jesus Christ. He is the Word of God, and He is the fulfillment of the Law: Perfect love manifested to the entire world. He loves us with a sacrificial, agape love. He laid down His life for us, and in turn, we can allow Him to live through us. We get to lay down our lives for Him and others.

Like a sketch gradually fading in order for the ultimate picture to form, we die to the law so that Christ might be revealed in and through us (Galatians 2:19).

Ephesians 5:1–2 says, "We are called to be imitators of God as dear children and walk in love, as Christ also has loved us and given Himself for us, an offering and a sacrifice to God for a sweet-smelling aroma." "By this we know love, that he laid down his life for us, and we ought to lay down our lives for the brothers" (1 John 3:16). "We love because He first loved us" (1 John 4:19). "For now we see in a mirror dimly, but then face to face. Now I know in part; then I shall know fully, even as I have been fully known" (1 Corinthians 13:12). "So now faith, hope, and love abide, these three; but the greatest of these is love" (1 Corinthians 13:13). "For we are his workmanship, created in Christ Jesus for good works, which God prepared beforehand, that we should walk in them" (Ephesians 2:10).

Jesus is the final image revealed. He is the picture that will last.

I encourage you to allow God to sketch His blueprint on your heart and conform you into the image of His Son, Jesus Christ (Romans 12:2, 8:29).

Obeying the Artist

I can recall battling with Jesus in my heart to trust Him. Although I said that He was my Lord and Savior, I struggled to give Him complete control of my life, even after He healed me. After being used to doing things my own way for so many years, it was a challenge for me to lay down my life before Him.

In my journey with Jesus, I started to recognize that my flesh was my worst enemy. I struggled with the power of sin—every sin you could possibly think of that I wasn't aware of before I received Him as my Lord and Savior.

Anger. Lust. Pride. And more.

I fought against the one who always wins. It was not easy. My flesh was strong and stubborn. It wanted what the Holy Spirit told me not to do.

Like He wrestled with Jacob, God wrestled with me (Genesis 32:22–32).

Over time, God's Word became stronger in my heart than my flesh.

My relationship with God continued in this manner until I could no longer do anything but submit and surrender to my Artist.

Then and only then could I finally find rest in Him.

Sound familiar?

As God's Art, we pretend we are the ones creating our lives, painting our days, writing our plans. Pride creeps into our hearts. Fear holds us back from trusting Him. Lust hides behind a pretty face.

But God is the One Who is recreating us in Christ. He sees the real us. He knows the dark parts of our hearts, and He desires to strip them away. When we meet Him at the cross, we are forgiven and transformed into the people He created us to be in Him.

Once He won me over, God gave me my new identity in Him.

As a new creation in Christ, God led me to the book of Esther in the Bible. Upon reading the story, I read about a disobedient woman named Vashti, who disobeyed the king in his palace.

"But Queen Vashti refused to come at the king's command delivered by the eunuchs. At this the king became enraged, and his anger burned within him" (Esther 1:12).

"According to the law, what is to be done to Queen Vashti, because she has not performed the command of King Ahasuerus delivered by the eunuchs?" (Esther 1:15).

"If it please the king, let a royal order go out from him, and let it be written among the laws of the Persians and the Medes so that it may not be repealed, that Vashti is never again to come before King Ahasuerus. And let the king give her royal position to another who is better than she" (Esther 1:19).

Eventually, Vashti was demoted. She was condemned in her sin. I realized then that the old, disobedient woman in me was overthrown by God. In Jesus Christ, I was no longer under the law, nor was I condemned in my sin. Vashti in me was put to death. That ugly enemy of God was subdued.

Thank God. Praise and glory to the One Who is strong and mighty to save.

It is God Who sketches His blueprint on our hearts, if we obey Him. He does this so that we can die to the law and live to Him. Then people can see and experience more of Christ, His life, in us.

The book of Esther is about an obedient woman. She was an orphan girl who eventually becomes the new queen to the King of Persia. In her state of humility, she was exalted to her royal position. Esther, who was "better than she," better than Vashti, was under grace (Esther 1:19). This new woman was under the submission of her king.

"The king loved Esther more than all the women, and she won grace and favor in his sight more than all the virgins, so that he set the royal crown on her head and made her queen instead of Vashti" (Esther 2:17).

Psalm 103:1–5 says, "Bless the Lord, O my soul, and all that is within me, bless his holy name! Bless the Lord, O my soul, and forget not all his benefits, who forgives all your iniquity, who heals all your diseases, who redeems your life from the pit, who crowns you with steadfast love and mercy, who satisfies you with good so that your youth is renewed like the eagle's."

"The Lord has established his throne in the heavens, and his kingdom rules over all. Bless the Lord, O you his angels, you mighty ones who do his word, obeying the voice of his word! Bless the Lord, all his hosts, his ministers, who do his will!" (Psalm 103:19–21).

In submission to Jesus Christ, I was now under His authority in His Kingdom. He became my Lord, and He ruled and reigned over me. I could now see Him and follow Him—His beauty and His light were all I wanted to see and reflect to the world.

His Art—His love—His image is what God desires to show others through His people.

Displaying His Art requires submission, an act of love in our hearts to obey the One Who made us, died for us, and rose from the grave for us.

Christ in us is the hope of glory (Colossians 1:27).

Obeying the Artist is a choice, and doing so is eternally worth it.

Will you decide to obey the One Who made you and is sovereign over all creation? If so, ask Him to help you turn your heart towards Him and His will for you.

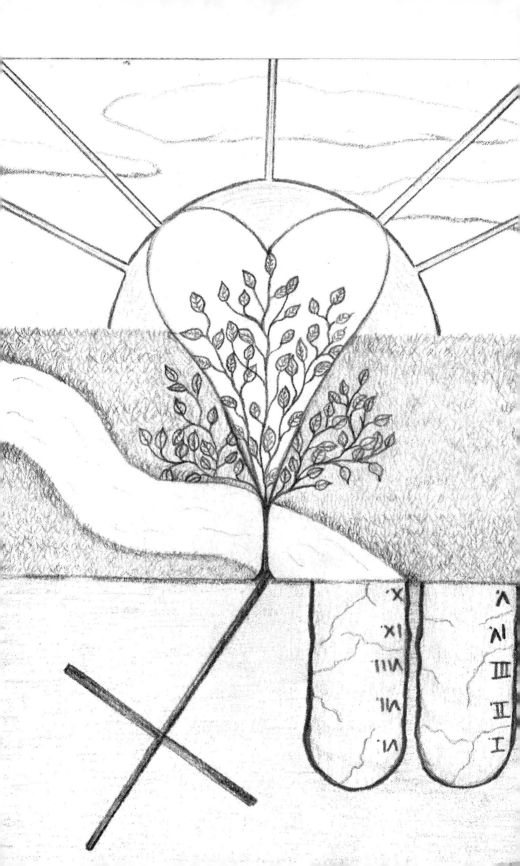

I was made to Love

I was made to love.
Not the kind of love our world drills into our minds.
Not the kind of love our world perverts to mankind.

You see, man looks at appearance.
We did from the beginning.
We fall for the lust of our eyes, for the lust of our flesh.
You see, without Him, we're just a mess.

Deceitful and fallen, wretched men we are without Him.
Playing with and hurting His beautiful creation.
We can't tell each other I love you when
we haven't received the truth.
We can't be faithful and honest when we haven't received His rest.

The man Christ Jesus, He's the only One we can trust.
With the joy set before Him, He endured the cross.
Bore our sins and our past, we can't look back.
He's the only one we truly have forever at last.

We were made to love, we were made to give.
But if we want true love, we have to submit.
You see, without Him, we can never know
Love as He intended it.

The kind of love that doesn't seek attention.
The kind of love that sees through a redemption.
The kind of love that hurts us and benefits them.
The kind of love that covers a multitude of sins.
The kind of love that never truly ends.

I was made to tell His story, the story of His love for humanity.
I'm just a messenger, a recipient of His mercy.
I'm like the Chief of Sinners; I'm the least of them all.
I should be dead, more than once came a fall.

He wrote it for our empty souls.
He wrote it for our broken hearts.
He wrote it for the Prisoner.
He wrote it for the one in the dark.

You're in a battle whether you know this or not.
Our first parents, Adam and Eve, chose to sin which led to death.
At our birth, we were sinful, prone to wander, prone to fall.
Like the first man and woman, we ignore God's call.

The pride of life, the lust of the flesh.
It's all over the world, it's in everything we possess.
The adultery and harlotry.
They drive us to insanity.

You see, we're slaves to these things.
We don't even know it.
They blind us into darkness.
And lead us to a pit.

But God has come to rescue us.
He loves us with a love I can't understand.
He's the Hero of His Story.
He came down from heaven and entered this land.

He was tempted by Satan.
Yet never once sinned.
He was perfect and faithful.
He resisted 'til the end.

God in the flesh, He went to the cross.
Died for our sins, to clean up our mess.
By His Holy Spirit, He rose from the dead.
Defeated Satan and cleared all your debt.

Believe on Him now and you'll be set free.
He did all of this for you and for me.
Don't you see?
God Himself has won the battle for eternity.

With His love, He did for us.
He conquered our enemy and promised us rest.
Believe on Him now and you'll be forgiven.
For you, precious soul, this gospel was written.

You see, this gospel is Alive.
He is Risen.
The Word became flesh.
It is finished.

Like the pen of a ready writer,
I tell His Story of His Love for Humanity.
His Love sets us free.
His Love is meant for you and for me.

The King of Love through us.
Only He can redeem our brokenness.
The King of Love in us.
Only He can fill our emptiness.

We were made to love.
The kind of love that doesn't seek attention.
The kind of love that sees through a redemption.
The kind of love that hurts us and benefits them.
The kind of love that covers a multitude of sins.
The kind of love that never truly ends.

 *Application*

God's love, whether you are conscious of it or not, pursues you. He is the great sacrifice made for you. He is the Greatest Lover, Friend, and Brother, as He laid down His life for us. For He did not come to be served, but to serve, and to give His life a ransom for many (Mark 10:45).

Perhaps, you are deciding to give Him your heart and accept Him as your Lord and Savior. If so, say a prayer like the one mentioned earlier, in your own words, from your heart to Him.

You might also be in a place where your heart is battling against His love. You may wonder if He is going to continue to love you, even though you have messed up and made mistakes. The answer is yes, but we should not tempt the Lord, our God. God's love is bigger than our mess and our mistakes. Trust Him.

Even if you can't feel His love, even if your heart is resisting His love right now, you can still be intentional in your heart to receive it.

Cling to God's promises for you. Hold onto them. Have faith. Trust in Jesus Christ as your personal Lord, Savior, Healer, and Redeemer. Know that God is your Artist Who is able to make all things new. It doesn't matter what your background is or who you are now. Jesus Christ can set you totally free to become who you were created to be in Him. With God's blueprint on your heart, you will be able to recognize His love when you see it and obey His Word when you hear it.

Read and Reflect

Romans 10:4: How is Christ the end of the law for righteousness?

_____

_____

_____

_____

_____

_____

_____

_____

Hebrews 10: Explain how the Old Testament is only a shadow of the things to come. What does Christ's coming mean for sinners?

_____

_____

_____

_____

_____

_____

_____

_____

Galatians 2:19–21: What does it mean to die to the law? How can you live to God?

_____

_____

_____

_____

_____

_____

_____

_____

Drawing Your Heart to Repentance

Line drawing is an art technique. The artist draws distinct lines, using dark and light pencils. To show a contrast between them, the artist draws dark lines to shade and draws light lines to highlight certain areas of an image.

The Bible says that without Christ, our minds and hearts are darkened (Ephesians 4:18; Romans 1:21). We are blinded to the things of God in our minds and hearts, bringing forth sinful and dark deeds (John 3:20; 2 Corinthians 4:4–6). In our sinful condition, all we can do is bear fruit that leads to death (Romans 6:23; Romans 7:15). We are a shaded image, walking in darkness.

This might sound somewhat tough to our ears, but it is also liberating to admit our need for a Savior in the dark. When we cannot see anything and have no idea where we are headed, it is comforting to know that there is a light in the world to rescue us. Jesus says that He can be our light and salvation. When we confess that we are utterly blind and lost, Jesus can be all we need. He can be our vision.

When we receive Jesus Christ as our Lord and Savior, He comes to dwell in our hearts (Ephesians 3:17; Romans 6:23). He gives life to the world (John 6:33). He gives light to the world and can shine on our darkness (Psalm 18:28, 119:130; John 1:9). In our hearts, Jesus Christ exposes our dark and evil intentions (Ephesians 5:13). He is the only One Who can lead us out of darkness into His marvelous light (1 Peter 2:9; Acts 26:18). Through His Word, He can enlighten our minds and hearts, and reveal God's good will to us (Ephesians 1:18; Romans 12:2). In Christ, we can be transformed into His image and bear fruit that leads to eternal life (2 Corinthians 3:18; John 15:16).

When God looks at the image before Him, He sees absolutely everything. Nothing is hidden from His sight. When He searches out His heartwork, the depths of our hearts, He convicts of us of our sin and draws us to repentance—out of darkness into His light. In this place, we are poor and needy, lost sinners in need of salvation. Our hearts are desperately wicked; we need Jesus. As His ransomed Art, it is important for us to submit to God's will for us, to turn from our sins and follow His ways. It is a battle to do so because we are accustomed to living and walking in sin.

When I initially came to Christ, I felt hurt, broken, and destroyed inside my heart and mind. Through recurring dreams, memories, and thoughts, my dark past haunted me. I had nightmares, horrible ones. I hardly slept and became suspicious of people and places that might have been good. Shame, resentment, bitterness, and fear crept into the dark corners of my heart and mind, and I didn't know what to do. I lived from these places and made decisions based on past failures and experiences. It was so difficult for my heart to leave the past behind and move forward. It was challenging for me to believe that I wasn't the sins I committed against God; I let people down in so many ways.

God was patient with me. Like a worn-out pencil in the Artist's hand, the darkness in me was gradually uncovered. Ultimately, God's lovingkindness drew me to repentance. He showed me acts of kindness and allowed me to make new decisions that honored Him. As I responded to His love, God continued to draw me near.

He continues to draw me. As we draw near to Him, He draws near to us (James 4:8).

Sometimes, we revisit the dark lines of our past for temporary relief. We falsely believe they can mask what we feel deep down inside—perhaps fear? Doubt? Insecurity? This only prolongs our deliverance from the sinful life that holds us back from walking in the light. As darkness was unveiled in me, I could begin to sense that my old sinful nature fought against all that God wanted for me. In this battle, all I could see was who I was and what I did before I met my Artist. I couldn't yet see who I was in Christ and what my Artist could make me in Him.

The Bible says that even after we come to Christ, we will be attacked by our enemies. We are in a spiritual war between light and dark principalities in the heavenly places (Ephesians 6). We are tempted to succumb to the temptations of Satan and return to our old sinful habits. We fight against Satan, the world, and our flesh. During this time, I struggled with depression, condemnation, and despair. God wanted to move me forward out of darkness, into His marvelous light. The enemy wanted me to remain in my sin and follow my own will. My flesh also wanted to do what I used to do.

But I learned this battle truly is the Lord's. Jesus says that if we want to be His disciples, we must deny ourselves, take up our cross, and follow Him daily (Matthew 16:24; Luke 9:23). With the help of the Holy Spirit, we must die to self and live to Christ. We must become nothing, so He can become our everything. Jesus Christ must be the Lord of our lives, and we must lose our life for Him to find it (Matthew 16:25–26). Then and only then can we have the light of life (John 8:12).

Surrendering to the Artist

Much of who we think we are derives from our past experiences—what we've done or what has been done to us. If we haven't filled our minds with the Word of God, our minds believe lies. If we haven't drenched our hearts with the truth, we listen to other voices besides our Good Shepherd's voice.

When I was delivered from lies within the New Age movement, Satan attacked me. When I was delivered from an unhealthy relationship, Satan condemned me. When I was pressured to do something I knew God didn't call me to do and I succumbed, I felt horrible.

For the next couple of years, Satan used my past to lie to me about who I was in Christ and keep me in bondage to certain sinful behaviors. During these times, I had destructive thoughts about myself and my future. Sometimes, I knew these thoughts were from the enemy. Other times, I blamed myself. People, places, and things reminded me of past memories I thought I already put away, out of my sight. But I guess I hadn't. I was stuck in these dark places.

While in spiritual warfare, I clung to God's Word. His Word began to renew my mind, heart, and soul.

One day, while I was driving on the road in my car, God spoke to my heart. He had brought me very far in my trust in Him, and I could feel our relationship had deepened.

That night, He asked me to trust Him even more.

It was dark, and I had no idea where I was going. I was supposed to meet my friend, but we had not decided where to meet. My phone died, so I couldn't call her or look up any directions on Google Maps. I didn't even know what my destination was at that point.

Then, I felt a nudge from God, saying, "Let me lead you." I was somewhat afraid, but by now, I knew I could trust Him to lead me.

So I did. I surrendered. I gave Him control of the wheel in my car.

The Holy Spirit led me. I had no vision of where I was going, but He became my vision.

He empowered me to move forward, to go where He was calling me to go.

I let go, and I let God.

My heart followed His lead.

Without any help from Google Maps or people, He brought me to exactly where I needed to be at the right time.

When I arrived at my destination, my friend wondered how I knew she was there.

I told her, "God led me."

Surrendering to my Artist, I realized, allowed Him to be Who He is: my God, my light, and my salvation.

In spite of your past, your present circumstances, and the unknown ahead of you, will you surrender to Jesus Christ? Will you allow Him to be your Lord and lead you in His footsteps?

Christ in You, the Hope of Glory

Tears break through your eyes,
a reflection of what's going on inside.
The cracks in your heart,
an inward mirror of your life falling apart.

Can we see hope in a state of brokenness?
Can we see light in a place of darkness?
Well, that's the promise of His story.
Jesus is the Way, the Savior of humanity.

Lost and fallen, you fight hard against the truth.
But the weight of sin becomes too heavy for you.
Like a woman forsaken and grieved in spirit,
you stand guilty before a crowd.
Like a man hurt and angry, you cave in and admit your faults.

Can we see hope in a state of brokenness?
Can we see light in a place of darkness?
Well, that's the promise of His story.
Jesus is the Way, the Savior of humanity.

You feel His tender love pull you close.
His bright light shines on your heart and starts to expose.
All that is dark, He removes and destroys.
All that is foreign, He evicts and slays.

Yeah, He can restore your heart to a state of wholeness.
He can make you a light in a place of darkness.
Yeah, this is the glorious riches of His mystery.
Christ in You, the hope of glory.

Yeah, He can turn your mourning into dancing.
He can give you new life and joy in the morning.
Yeah, this is the glorious riches of His mystery.
Christ in you, the hope of glory.

 **Application**

You might be struggling to leave the dark. It might still feel very comfortable. It could be that you are battling depression, condemnation, or despair. It could be an addiction or a person God has asked you to break away from at this time. It could even be a relationship you know you should not be in right now. Please know that you are not alone. Jesus is with you. If you are hanging out in the shadows, accustomed to darkness, God is faithful to deliver you. If you have been hurt, broken, or destroyed inside, know that God loves you right where you are right now. As your Artist, He can take the broken pieces of your soul and make you whole in Him. He desires to bring you into His marvelous light.

Being abused, deceived, or violated in your heart, mind, and body is not right in God's sight (Psalm 72:12–14). Being taken advantage of or oppressed by someone in power because of your vulnerable position is insulting to God (Proverbs 14:31). God sees everything, and justice belongs to Him. The Bible says that vengeance is God's (Romans 12:19). He rescues the oppressed. He will punish the world for its evil and the wicked for their iniquity. He will put an end to the arrogance of the haughty and will humble the pride of the ruthless (Isaiah 13:11). At the end of God's story, the devil will be thrown into the lake of fire and brimstone, with the beast and the false prophet, and they will be tormented day and night forever (Revelation 20:10).

Even if you do not feel this truth in your heart yet, know that Jesus Christ came to earth for you, specifically. He lived the perfect life you could never live here. He died on the cross for your sins and your enemies' sins. The first step you can take to heal any wounds in your heart, mind, and soul is to receive Jesus Christ into your heart. Receive God's forgiveness for your sins. Trust that He is good. He loves you with an everlasting love. With lovingkindness, God draws you to Himself (Jeremiah 31:3). He is the Father to the fatherless and a defender of widows (Psalm 68:5).

Second, read God's Word. The Bible will give you a hunger and thirst for Him; it will help you die to self and live by faith in Him (Galatians 2:20). Through His Holy Spirit, God will begin to enlighten your heart and mind. He will start to open your spiritual eyes and lead you out of darkness into His marvelous light. It might feel uncertain at times, but God knows what He is doing and where He is taking you; the cross is our resting place, where we are humbled, forgiven, and set free. There, darkness fades; light invades. Jesus, we see, is all we need.

Jeremiah 31:3: How does God's lovingkindness lead us to repentance?

_____
_____
_____
_____
_____
_____
_____

Romans 2:4: How are you responding to God's goodness towards you?

_____
_____
_____
_____
_____
_____
_____

Ephesians 4:32: Forgiveness is freeing for the person forgiving and the person being forgiven. Do you know you are forgiven by God? Who do you need to forgive?

_____
_____
_____
_____
_____
_____

Molding and Shaping Your Heart

The Bible says that God is our Potter. We are the work of His hands (Isaiah 64:8). Just as a Potter would press a lump of clay into his hands to mold and shape it, God presses us into Him. We are challenged to "count it all joy, my brothers, when you meet trials of various kinds, for you know that the testing of your faith produces steadfastness" (James 1:2–3). During difficult times in our lives, we are called to depend on Jesus. We must look to Jesus, the author and finisher of our faith, who for the joy set before Him endured the cross, despising the shame, and sat down at the right hand of the throne of God (Hebrews 12:2). We are hard-pressed on every side, but not crushed; perplexed, but not in despair; persecuted, but not abandoned; struck down, but not destroyed (2 Corinthians 4:9).

Like clay is shaped in an artist's hands, we are shaped in God's hands. When we struggle on our walk of faith with Him, He does not let us go. He holds onto us and presses us towards Him. Even when we are faithless, He remains faithful, for He cannot deny Himself (2 Timothy 2:13). When we are transported into a fiery situation, like clay is transported into a kiln, the Lord does not leave us or forsake us (1 Peter 1:7; Daniel 3:25). He stands right by our side and watches over us. The Bible says that God never sleeps (Psalm 121:2–4). Sometimes, when we are going through trials, we may feel that God has left us. During these times, we may think He does not love us. But this is not true. He is there with us, omnipresent. One of God's names is Jehovah-Shammah, which means "The Lord is there" in Hebrew.[11]

We are called to maintain our faith in Christ during this period (1 Timothy 6:12). "So that the tested genuineness of your faith—more precious than gold that perishes though it is tested by fire—may be found to result in praise and glory and honor at the revelation of Jesus Christ" (1 Peter 1:7). In this process, God is molding and shaping us into the image of His Son, Jesus Christ. Even if we don't feel Him, we must trust God and the goodness of His Heart for us. He knows what He is doing with His creation. We are mere dust (Psalm 103:14). We can't always see our circumstances through the eternal perspective of our God. This is why we need to stand on God's Word, no matter how we feel or what we perceive on earth.

---

[11] https://biblehub.com/topical/j/jehovah-shammah.htm

Clinging to the Artist

After I confessed that Jesus Christ was my Lord and savior, God allowed me to go through several trials, one after another.

I had already destroyed my plans for my life.

My career, my love life, my dreams were broken, dead.

My finances, my possessions were lost.

One day, while I was rock climbing at the gym, I fell, breaking my tibula and fibula bones and fracturing my ankle. My right foot was dislocated and needed immediate surgery. In this same season, I got a horrible infection in my cheek, and it swelled up tremendously. When I glanced at myself in the mirror, I saw several disfigured and broken pieces of myself before me.

My leg and face were shattered. Grief and loss from the deaths of loved ones still lingered in my heart. Shame, guilt, and anger from being deceived in the New Age movement still possessed my heart. My identity seemed, well, stolen from me during this time. I felt bitter about my past. I missed my old friends. They gradually left, one by one, after I confessed Jesus Christ as my Lord and Savior. I was a mess.

Plus, I was an adult in my late twenties, living back at home with my dad.

From the world's perspective, I lost everything.

For the next year, I walked with crutches and an oversized boot for my foot. I was truly torn apart from the inside out. Yet with the help of His Holy Spirit, the Lord drew me closer to Him at this time. Like a lost and broken lamb, I clung to my Good Shepherd. He carried me and began to show me who He was and what I needed—Him (Isaiah 40:11).

God wasn't interested in my physical appearance as much as He was with the inside of my heart.

God wanted to reshape my disfigured, empty, and broken heart. I was a hopeless and lost sinner, but the Lord had mercy on me. He was with me during this season and through so many more trials. When I made mistakes, He never condemned me. To this day, I am amazed by God's wisdom in allowing His Art to be pressed, tested, and tried. Like any artist, God isn't interested in creating anything fake or phony. He makes His Art genuine, so it lasts (1 Corinthians 3:11–15, 13:13).

In the meantime, the spiritual war I was in against the enemy escalated.

God humbled me. Like a potter with his clay, He threw me on His wheel and molded me. He saw many cracks in me and brought me to fiery places, where my faith was tested.

When difficult times arose in my past, my tendency was to run away from home to faraway places. I traveled. I escaped. I hung out with the outcasts, those who I knew were different. They were runaways, like me.

But now, I couldn't.

I couldn't hide from God.

I could kick and scream, or I could cling to Him. He knew where I was, always.

I chose to cling to Him. The more I did, the more I started to reflect His character.

It is not easy for our hearts to cling to our Artist. We want to jump off the Potter's wheel, run away, and leave Him. We want to return to the world, the comfort zone of the flesh. But as long as you are honest with God, He will meet you exactly where you are at and handle you with care.

In light of eternity, it is far better to hold onto our Artist than turn to the world and remain in deception. If I did not give my broken heart to Jesus and wait on God to have His way, I would not have been set free to serve Him wholeheartedly.

His plan is better than anything we've ever imagined. We need to believe Him.

Clinging to our Artist is what we need to do, over and over again. He is helping us to be more like Him and preparing us for heaven.

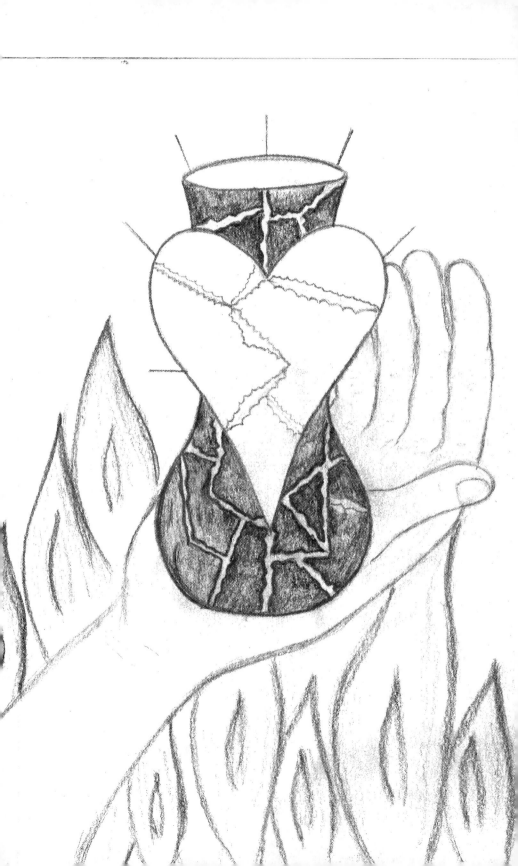

Guard My Heart

In my heart, we speak the truth.
In my heart, I'll follow You.
In my heart, we praise Your name.
In my heart, I'll wait for strength.

Will you guard my heart
from the enemy's lies?
From the fiery darts?
From the fears and the doubts?

In my heart, we speak the truth.
In my heart, I'll follow You.
In my heart, we praise Your name.
In my heart, I'll wait for strength.

Will you guard my heart
from the enemy's traps?
From my ghostly past?
From the tears and attacks?

In my heart, we speak the truth.
In my heart, I'll follow You.
In my heart, we praise Your name.
In my heart, I'll wait for strength.

 **Application**

Perhaps you are in a season of testing or of brokenness and mourning over the sins of your past. God is trying your faith. You are in the fire. I exhort you, as you are pressed in these circumstances, turn to Jesus. Do not walk away from Him. Do not turn to the world for help. Go to God. Spend time with Him and know that He is in control (Psalm 46:10). Wait patiently for Him and cling to Him (Deuteronomy 13:4). If you do, you will come out of your fiery trial looking more like Him. Though it may be uncomfortable, Jesus is directing you towards Him. He knows exactly what He is doing and knows all of your ways (Psalm 139).

Do not give up. Be encouraged. Make changes in your life where things do not align with His will. Let go of your past. Move forward. Stay faithful to Jesus and fight the good fight of faith (1 Timothy 6:12). When He takes you out of the fire, your faith will be more genuine. By God's gracious hand, you will be made more shiny and beautiful from the inside out. Though we begin as marred vessels in the Potter's hand, He can make us into another vessel as it seems good for Him to make (Jeremiah 18:4; 2 Timothy 2:21; Romans 9:21).

Isaiah 64:8: Who is the Potter? Who is the clay? What can He do with His clay?

_____
_____
_____
_____
_____
_____
_____

Jeremiah 18:4: What was the condition of the clay in the Potter's hands? What did the Potter do with it?

_____
_____
_____
_____
_____
_____
_____

2 Timothy 2:21: What does God instruct us to do? What will the result be if we do what He says?

_____
_____
_____
_____
_____
_____
_____

Purifying Your Heart

God, as our Artist, purifies His Art like a refiner purifies gold. Gold looks beautiful and valuable to the average person, but before it is made into jewelry, it undergoes a process of cleansing. God sees flaws and impurities in our character and desires to extract ungodly attitudes in our hearts. He wants to develop godly qualities in us. He sees the potential in us to become more like His Son, Jesus Christ, and so He takes us through a process of refinement. Through trials in our lives, God also leads us from repentance to sanctification; from a life of sin to a life of obedience. After this process, God can see more of His Son in our hearts, shining for His glory. Ultimately, He wants our hearts to shine like gold.

As sinners, we need to recognize that we are impure with sin (Isaiah 64:6). The more we seek Christ, the more we see the impurities and imperfections that still exist in us. We sinners are guilty. Of selfishness? Yes. Of envy? Yes. Of pride? Yes. To these acts, we are called to die (Galatians 5:19–21; Colossians 2:20). The perverse in heart are an abomination to the Lord (Proverbs 11:20). The crucible for silver and the furnace for gold, but the Lord tests the heart (Proverbs 17:3). So God calls us to purify ourselves (1 John 3:3; James 4:8; 2 Corinthians 7:1). He commands that we put off our old ways and make no provision for the flesh (Romans 8:13, 12:1, 13:14). We must die to the law and live to Him (Galatians 2:19). When we do, we suffer the loss of things, people, or jobs for the sake of Christ

(Philippians 3:7). God says that if our hand causes us to stumble, we need to cut if off (Mark 9:43). We must be crucified with Christ and live by faith in Him (Galatians 2:20).

The Bible says that the elements of the world will be destroyed with intense heat, and the earth and its works will be burned up (2 Peter 3:10–12). When our hearts are under intense heat, we can cry out to God, "Thy will be done." We can trust that His ways are best for us. Colossians 2:8 says, "See to it that no one takes you captive by philosophy and empty deceit, according to human tradition, according to the elemental spirits of the world, and not according to Christ." There are so many different ideas, habits, and ways of the world that are empty and useless in our minds and hearts. God wants us to get rid of them and align ourselves with His will. Only what is built upon Christ will truly last. This means that we must develop a heart and mindset that is Christ-like.

Only God can take us through this process of refinement. We must surrender our hearts to Him and allow Him to have His way with us. We must decrease, and He must increase (John 3:30). Only God knows our true motives, and He desires to set us free from the weak and worthless elementary principles of the world (Galatians 4:9). For "all flesh is like grass and all its glory like the flower of grass. The grass withers, and the flower falls, but the word of the Lord remains forever. And this word is the good news that was preached to you" (1 Peter 1:24–25). James 4:8 says, "Draw near to God, and he will draw near to you. Cleanse your hands, you sinners, and purify your hearts, you double-minded."

Cooperating with the Artist

One day, the Holy Spirit whispered to my heart about bitterness I was holding onto against my stepmom, Grace. He used another sister in Christ to expose bitterness and pride in my heart. Prior to God revealing this to me, I was not aware of these dark roots of bitterness and pride growing on the inside of my heart. For a few moments, I struggled to receive the truth about myself.

Deep inside my soul, I thought of what was done to me rather than my own sin.

God immediately confronted me and said, "That's pride."

Sitting alone with God in my '94 Honda Accord on a cold, dark night, I struggled with the truth about my own heart. I knew my Artist was right. I felt Him ask me to let go of these ungodly thoughts and attitudes.

"I can't do it," I told Jesus. I felt like a prisoner again, sitting in my own prison cell.

There was no way out of what I felt in my heart. It was ugly. I couldn't stand what I felt deep within me, but I also battled to release it.

Jesus spoke to my heart again: "If you say that I am your King and you want to be used for my glory, you must submit to me."

King? Well, yes, I did proclaim He was my King. I did want Him to use me for His glory.

I was so convicted by His statement.

"Why is this so hard for me to give You?" I felt like a captive soul restrained by heavy chains, unable to obey Him.

I broke into tears. My fists clenched. The bitterness in me lied dormant—there in the center of my heart. It felt as if it controlled me. The more I became aware of it, the fouler it became. It was an impurity that was out in the open, for my Artist to see. It must have looked monstrous.

"Obey me," Jesus said.

I couldn't do it. I fought against His command.

"Help me," I cried. "Take over."

I took a deep breath and sighed. I was told I wasn't a slave to my sin any longer, but at that moment, I felt like one. For some reason, perhaps because of His love for prisoners like myself, Jesus waited for me to cooperate with Him.

In my heart, I finally decided to obey Him.

"Have your way," I cried. "Help me."

Suddenly, old, repressed tears streamed out of my eyes, like healing water washing out an open wound. I didn't know how hurt I was for so many years. I was so hurt. "Hurt" comes from the root word, *chabal* in Hebrew.[12] It means "injury." Now, I could feel that the injury in my heart was deep, unattended for many years. In a matter of seconds, I also became aware of the unkind and hostile attitudes I carried in my heart; they didn't allow my heart to breathe, let alone sing or dance. I was bitter, and I needed forgiveness.

"You're right, God," I confessed to Him. "I'm wrong. I have held onto this bitterness all this time."

---

[12] https://biblehub.com/str/hebrew/2257.htm

The Lord encouraged me in that moment to apologize to Grace for all of the wrong I committed over the years.

Still in tears, I unquestioningly grabbed my cell phone. The strength of the Lord rested upon me as I confessed to her, "I'm sorry for …" As I uttered these words to her, my wounded heart began to breathe a sigh of relief. I gasped and hiccupped, as the monster in me departed.

Humility and repentance—what I fought against for so long, I learned—would lead me to freedom.

As God's power of forgiveness worked in me, my heart began to feel soft and sensitive, as if Jesus' healing hands were covering hidden bruises found in the deep recesses of my soul. He was peeling away these ugly, dark roots out of my heart that He knew did not belong there anymore. His love gradually touched parts of me that were guarded for most of my life. Though I could hide them from people, I could not keep them from Him.

Ahhhh. Like a prisoner being set free from her dark and cold cell, I inhaled the breath of life in me once again.

Jesus.

When I did allow Jesus to heal me, I felt and tasted holiness. He was purifying me, and I felt better, newer, and cleaner. The bitterness in me was gone. Jesus washed and cleansed me.

A couple of days later, Grace and I met up for breakfast. As we sat across from each other, I felt clear. My heart felt blameless before her. There was nothing but God's love between us now, and I knew this was a miracle!

His Grace. It was sufficient.

Sitting next to us were my five-year-old niece and her mom, my sister. Coincidently, they attended a church service the previous weekend and learned about the story of the Good Samaritan.

"Tell her about the story of the Good Samaritan," my sister prompted her daughter.

"Jesus heals our *cocos*," my niece sweetly uttered as she shared the story of the Good Samaritan with us (*cocos* is slang in Spanish for "bruises").

I looked at my niece with gratitude and agreed, "Amen. Yes, He does."

Jesus heals the brokenhearted and binds up their wounds (Psalm 147:3). Through her reminder of His Word, I realized that I was touched by Jesus, the Good Samaritan.

He healed my cocos. I had deep cocos. Ugly cocos. Monstrous cocos, what I thought were unreachable for Jesus.

Like a dream come true, I could see God's compassionate Heart for the hurting, and it was beautiful.

If you know you have cocos that God is revealing in your heart, will you allow Him to touch and heal you? It might feel painful at first, but it is so worth it when the Great Physician visits us.

In our prison cell.

At our doctors' appointments.

On our hospital bed.

As He sets us free, heals our hearts, and binds up our wounds, He makes all things new and beautiful.

The Great Physician

His scarred hands heal our broken souls.
He searches deep within and makes us whole.
His light shines on every battered scar.
His blood covers every darkened part.

When we've seen the Great Physician,
our hearts are forever changed.
We are new creations in Christ. He gives us a new name.
We are healed. We are restored.
We are cleansed. We are adored.
The soul who trusts in Him is blessed forevermore.

Jesus is your Great Physician.
He's the One Who heals your scars.
Jesus is your Good Samaritan.
He's the One Who mends your heart.

He was pierced for your transgressions.
He was bruised for your iniquities.
He was hurt for all your shortcomings.
He was struck for all your infirmities.

Trust in His gentle touch.
Let Him pull you close.
His light will shine on all your wounds.
His blood will make you whole.

Jesus is your Great Physician.
He's the One Who heals your scars.
Jesus is your Good Samaritan.
He's the One Who mends your heart.

Trust in His gentle touch.
Let Him pull you close.
His light will shine on all your wounds.
His blood will make you whole.

Jesus.
He is the Great Physician.
Jesus.
He died for all our sins.

Jesus.
He is the Good Samaritan.
Jesus.
His blood was shed for all our sins.

Jesus is your Great Physician.
He's the One Who heals your scars.
Jesus is your Good Samaritan.
He's the One Who mends your heart.

Trust in His gentle touch.
Let Him pull you close.
His light will shine on all your wounds.
His blood will make you whole.

Application

Like an artist melts gold in intense heat to remove its impurities, God may have you in a refining furnace, applying heat to your heart so you can be purified. If so, surrender to the Lord. Trust Him. Wait on Him. He knows when to take you out of the furnace and scrape off everything that does not look like Him. "If we confess our sins, he is faithful and just to forgive us our sins and to cleanse us from all unrighteousness" (1 John 1:9).

If you want to be a follower of Jesus Christ, you must choose to forgive those who hurt you in the past and ask for forgiveness for whatever you have done to them. You must learn to say no to the pressures of the world and yes to God's will. In receiving God's grace, you can give grace to those who need it.

 *Read and Reflect*

James 1: What are we to do when we find ourselves in a trial? What does the testing of our faith produce in us?

_____
_____
_____
_____
_____
_____
_____
_____

1 Peter 5:10: What does God do after you've endured suffering?

_____
_____
_____
_____
_____
_____
_____

Luke 10:25–37: In contrast to everyone else, what did the Good Samaritan do with the wounded heart?

_____
_____
_____
_____
_____
_____

Capturing Your Heart

Photographers are visual artists. To capture an image, they use a camera, which records light onto it.[13] Essentially, they draw with light. If someone takes your photo, you may see a light flash before your eyes. The light captures and draws the image in a matter of milliseconds.

For most of my life, I wanted to feel beautiful when a photo was being taken of me. As a woman, I wanted to look free. But every time I stood in front of a camera, I felt as if I needed to hide something, something beneath me in my heart—shame, fear, or sadness. I didn't want anyone to see the true colors (or lack thereof) in my heart, so I made sure to put a fictitious mask on around photographers. When they asked to take my picture, I fake smiled. Over the years, I became good at looking happy, even though I wasn't. My eyes, though opened, were closed in my heart. My eyes, though opened, were blinded in my heart. There was darkness. For many years, I put up a front, and everyone but the Lord Himself—the true light—assumed that I was fine.

One day after God did an incredible work in my heart, destroying some of my ugly, dark, and ungodly attitudes, He gave me the opportunity to see what He did. Walking into the art studio where

---

[13] https://www.britannica.com/technology/photography

I worked at the time, I bumped into my boss' Pastor, who happened to be a photographer.

"Take a picture with me," my boss said. My hair wasn't done, and my outer appearance totally didn't reflect what I wanted to look like in a picture.

I hesitated.

"You're fine," my boss said. "Come take one with me."

"Okay," I consented.

As I scooted closer to my boss to take a picture, the photographer noticed something on my arm.

"You have some ashes on your arm," he noted.

Ashes? I looked at my arm. Dark ashes were spread over my skin. *How did they get there?* I wondered.

Then I recalled: a few minutes earlier, I was in the parking lot and found a branch underneath my car. The ashes must have gotten on me when I removed the branch.

"Oh," I said aloud. "They're from underneath my car when I removed this branch."

"Take them off," my boss and the photographer instructed.

Dusting the ashes off my arm, God spoke to my heart, "I turned your ashes into beauty."

Right away, this statement popped into my mind, "From death to life, from ashes to beauty, my God is bringing me from glory to glory." This had been a motto I recited to God when we first began our journey together. I could feel the transformation that God did in my heart. My inner self was different, renewed. I no longer felt shame, hate, fear, depression, or anger weighing me down. I had lived with them for so long, but now they were gone. It was a miracle. *Christ in me*, I thought, *the hope of glory. This is a miracle. He is the miracle. He is the light of the world.* I could feel the eyes of my heart open wide, and for the first time in front of a camera, they were smiling. My heart was smiling. It was free.

The ashes were off my arm now, and I stood next to my boss, ready for our picture. I was unashamed. The photographer lifted up his camera, and a light flashed before my eyes. My heart—my heart—my heart was so happy! My heart could reflect His love. Jesus was in my heart, shining. The light from the camera shone against His light, and I could breathe deeply within my soul. As if Jesus' hands were enlarging my heart from within for all to see, I could sense His grace fill me and expand in me.

"God did a work in your heart," the photographer noted.

I could only imagine what he must have seen before my transformation—darkness? Now, he could see the risen Jesus Christ, our Lord and Savior, in me.

"Yes, He did," I declared.

I was so grateful. I could take no credit for God's handiwork. He is the ultimate photographer. He reflects His light and captures His light in us. So "all the world could see our good works and glorify our Father in heaven" (Matthew 5:16).

Jesus broke through my darkness. God's unconditional love reached past the sin I carried deep inside my heart. He broke through and reached past the darkness in me because He is Light. Jesus Christ dispels the dark, and He remains, His beauty for everyone to see.

Believing the Artist

Sometimes, when we have been so hurt in our past, it is difficult to believe in God's love for us personally. Because of what we've gone through, we are accustomed to hiding behind protective walls we build up around our hearts. Our hearts have been broken, bruised, and disappointed. So we operate from places of hurt.

My past produced nothing but death.

But …

If we give our hearts just as they are to Jesus, He is faithful to heal and mend them.

If we believe in Him, He can deliver us from darkness and give us light.

He can break down our walls and enter into our hearts—to stay there, to deliver us from our chains.

He does not leave us, nor does He forsake us.

He comforts us.

He counsels us.

He encourages us.

He fights for us.

He defends us.

He overcomes our enemies, even ourselves.

Your heart may feel hard right now. You may have built up many walls in your heart to survive in this world. But if you continue to allow Jesus into your heart and surrender to Him, He can change everything. He can transform you.

He is able to do this, not because of who we are, but because of Who He is and what He's done for us on the cross.

He is the love we need.

He is the miracle we believe in, now and forever. He rose from the dead.

He is alive, and the power that raised Jesus from the grave is now living in His believers.

He is our future.

We must continue to believe, wait, and see.

Life is better in Him.

Do you believe this?

Let His Face Shine Upon You

He is the light in the dark.
He is the joy when it's grey.
He is the peace in the storm.
He is the comfort when we mourn.

Let His face shine upon you.
May His grace cover you.
Let His face shine upon you.
May His grace cover you.

He is the Father who never leaves.
He is the Lover who fills our needs.
He is the God who never slumbers.
He is the Friend who remembers.

Let His face shine upon you.
May His grace cover you.
Let His face shine upon you.
May His grace cover you.

Oh His love. He is love.
Oh His love. He is love.

Let His face shine upon you.
May His grace cover you.
Let His face shine upon you.
May His grace cover you.

When we meet Him, we shall be like Him.
Be like Him, be like Him.
When we meet Him, we shall be like Him.
Be like Him, be like Him.

Oh His love. He is love.
Oh His love. He is love.

Let His face shine upon you.
May His grace cover you.
Let His face shine upon you.
May His grace cover you.

 **Application**

Isaiah 61:1–3 says, "The Spirit of the Lord God is upon me, because the Lord has anointed me to bring good news to the poor; he has sent me to bind up the brokenhearted, to proclaim liberty to the captives, and the opening of the prison to those who are bound; to proclaim the year of the Lord's favor, and the day of vengeance of our God; to comfort all who mourn; to grant to those who mourn in Zion—to give them a beautiful headdress instead of ashes, the oil of gladness instead of mourning, the garment of praise instead of a faint spirit; that they may be called oaks of righteousness, the planting of the Lord, that he may be glorified."

Sometimes, we hear the words "God loves you," but we do not believe them. All we can feel is darkness. We see people at church with big smiles on their faces and think that because we do not feel happy, we must not belong there. We believe the lies that we could never be good enough, like everyone else; we are not joyful. So we settle. We remain in darkness. We settle for broken relationships, drug use, abuse, or self-righteousness to hide the gloom in our hearts. We stay in these places of shame, hate, fear, depression, and anger. We return to our old life before we received Jesus Christ as our Lord and Savior and hide. We hang out in the prison of our hearts and mourn. We carry a spirit of heaviness; sometimes, like I did for a long time, we fake smile.

I want to remind you that Jesus is with you, to give you good news. He is with you, in the dark place of your broken heart, to heal it. He proclaims freedom over your heart. He is the One Who opens your captive heart. He accepts you in Him. He comforts you and consoles you. He loves you unconditionally, regardless of what you have done in your past. He forgives you. On the cross, Jesus said, "Father, forgive them, for they know not what they do." And they cast lots to divide His garments (Luke 23:34).

Vengeance is God's. He will give you beauty for ashes and joy for your mourning. He will give you a garment of praise for your spirit of heaviness. Your name will reflect a tree of righteousness. It will be His planting, so that He is glorified.

If you are in a place of brokenness, and your heart and mind are being hurt, used, or abused in any manner, look to Jesus Christ. He loves you and treats you with lovingkindness. You are God's precious creation, and He has a plan of salvation for you in His Son, Jesus Christ. Jesus is the Healer of humanity. Let the Prince of Peace rescue you, hold you, and keep you for Himself for all of eternity.

In your heart, God truly does say, "I love you." His love speaks over the deceiving voices of the enemy. His love helps you to let your guard down completely and surrender to His rule over you. The physical masks over your heart are destroyed. The phoniness that fooled everyone else in the world is gone. Jesus calls your name and knows you. He sees through your heart and finds you—the real you, unconditionally loved. His love promises you a different picture for your heart. The heat of His light warms your heart, and you are accepted in Him, the Beloved.

Wherever you stand right now, trust in God's love and let His light capture the eyes of your heart for all of eternity. He will take your heart to places you have never imagined, and you will see His glory.

Like He promised me, He promises you: from death to life; from ashes to beauty; He will bring you from glory to glory.

 *Read and Reflect*

John 9:35–10:21: Do you believe in the Son of God?

_____

_____

_____

_____

_____

_____

_____

_____

Ephesians 1:18–23: What is Paul's prayer for us?

_____

_____

_____

_____

_____

_____

_____

_____

Luke 24:13–35: What did the disciples discover on the road to Emmaus?

_____

_____

_____

_____

_____

_____

_____

Softening Your Heart

Before Jesus started to heal me, my heart was tough, like a hard lump of clay. I must have felt impossible to work with and use in the Potter's hands. I was hurt, offended, and defensive about my past. No matter how much I tried in my own strength, I couldn't seem to open up my heart to Jesus' healing touch. I wanted to be healed and cried out to Him nearly every night.

Perhaps you feel this way now. Many of us have been traumatized by certain experiences we have gone through in life and cannot seem to trust in the Lord with all of our hearts (Proverbs 3:4–7). We are afraid to get hurt again. We are defensive and suspicious of God and other people.

Why did You allow this to happen? you think in your heart to God, referring to a tragic experience you went through years ago.

Why did You let them say those mean things to me? Why did You allow me to be deceived for so long? Why did You let him die? These words, if not uttered from our mouths, may be in our hearts.

God is a big God. He is our Father. You might think these thoughts are rude, and you are right. They are not respectful. But for me and for you, they might be real.

God, I have learned, can soften the hardness of our hearts. With His love, He leads us to follow Him. He promises that He works everything together for good for those who love Him and are called according to His purpose (Romans 8:28). Genesis 50:20 says, "As for you, you meant evil against me, but God meant it for good, to bring it about that many people should be kept alive, as they are today."

Though I could not always feel God's handiwork in my heart, I trusted that He was helping me to heal. After releasing old, repressed tears from my eyes and asking Him to help me forgive others and myself, God revealed His handprints were all over my heart. I not only asked for forgiveness from Grace; God helped me to ask for forgiveness from (and forgive) many others. When the old tears from my internal hurts were wiped away, a new person emerged. It was Christ in me; it was His love and forgiveness in me.

One day, while I was working at the art studio, a female customer commented to me, "You're very soft." She, on the other hand, seemed a bit tough and cynical in her demeanor.

Soft? I was so taken aback by her comment.

The woman shared with me that she was struck by my feminine voice, character, and approach towards others.

I was shocked. *Me? Soft? Glory to God,* I thought.

Then, it dawned on me. *The world makes girls hard.* I suddenly realized the work of God in me.

"The world often makes girls tough and hard as they grow up and experience disappointments, sorrow, or tragedy," I said to the woman.

Over time, many women become guarded, callous, or cynical towards God, themselves, and others. They have been hurt by so many people and experiences. It is no surprise that women in the world are the way they are today. The world all around us reflects an image that we unconsciously adopt for survival reasons.

This tough, independent, and selfish woman ends up guarded, callous, and cynical towards God, herself, and others. But deep inside, she is hurting. She has wounds that have been unattended.

This was me.

"God originally created females to be gentle and soft," I told her. "The only reason I am soft now is because of my decision to accept Jesus Christ into my heart. He was and is a gentleman. He healed me. God is a good Father."

"I am who I am now because of God's grace in me," I continued.

A few moments later, my boss asked me, "Can you please help me mix these lumps of clay together? Some of them are hard and some of them are soft. We need to mix them together."

In order for a hard lump of clay to become soft, I learned, the Potter needs to mix them together.

God spoke to my heart at that moment and said, "You look soft to her because I am soft, gentle, and lowly at heart. You are united to me now." As the two lumps of clay are meshed and molded into one lump, they become one. They are softened together. Then, the Potter can use them to make something beautiful.

The customer watched me as I mixed the two lumps of clay together. Silently, I hoped and prayed that one day, she could see that Jesus could be a gentleman to her too.

When we put on Christ and obey His ways, we are molded into His image. When we learn of Him and spend time with Him, we can become more like Him. God's goodness and lovingkindness lead us to repentance. His forgiveness leads us to forgive. His kindness leads us to be kind. His love leads us to love. His generosity leads us to be generous.

The word "soft" in Hebrew is *rak*. It can also mean "tender, delicate, refined."[14]

If God could take a hurt, broken, and hard girl like me and make her soft, He's got to be the best Artist of the human heart.

I am so grateful for His patience with aching hearts. Sometimes, I wonder how He could see the potential for redemption in a soul who

---

[14] https://biblehub.com/hebrew/7390.htm

has gone through so much tragedy. You might have experienced a lot of harm and disappointment in your life, and you wonder if God can do this same work in you. God can; He sees differently than we see ourselves. God sent Jesus Christ into a dark world to seek and save the lost, to heal the brokenhearted, and to turn them into new creations in Him, prepared and ready to walk in newness of life (Romans 6:4). In Him, we can walk as children of light (Ephesians 5:8). With man, this is impossible, but with God all things are possible (Matthew 19:26).

Following the Artist

Every year, a live art show called *Pageant of the Masters* is held in Laguna Beach, California. I attended it as a believer, and as I sat watching it, God spoke to my heart. I did not know why He led me to see this show, until the end of it.

On stage, a painting came to life. The painting demonstrated the life of a female artist, whose entire life consisted of vanity. She had everything, including a man, fame, and money. But at the end of her life, she remained heartbroken. Her story ended in sadness, sorrow, and death. It was devastating.

Far in the back row of the bleachers, I sat watching this painting in action, listening to her story.

"I don't want my life to end that way," I told God in my heart. I wanted to follow Him.

"Then Jesus said to his disciples, 'Whoever wants to be my disciple must deny themselves and take up their cross and follow me. For whoever wants to save their life will lose it, but whoever loses their life for me will find it. What good will it be for someone to gain the whole world, yet forfeit their soul? Or what can anyone give in exchange for their soul?'" (Matthew 16:24–26).

At the very end of the art show, the famous painting called *The Last Supper* by Leonardo da Vinci came to life. This painting demonstrated the life of Jesus Christ, whose entire life was perfect. Right before my eyes, I saw that He laid down His life for His friends. I saw the Bread of Life before me. He was going to the cross. He was at the table, offering Himself.

Then, I silently cried out to God in my heart, "God, I don't want to be like that woman who ended her life without You. I don't want to live life without You. I want You. I need You. You're the Master Artist!"

And I knew in that moment, I needed to die with Christ. I was thirsty for the living water and hungry for the Bread of Life. I was called to drink His blood. I wanted Him to become my all and all. I needed to deny myself, take up my cross, and follow Him (Matthew 16:24).

Thereafter, God became my Master Artist. Following the Master Artist has not been easy, but He is my everything: eternal Life; my all and all.

I have been crucified with Christ, and I no longer live, but Christ lives in me. The life I now live in the body, I live by faith in the Son of God, Who loved me and gave Himself for me (Galatians 2:20).

He's Knocking on the Door of Your Heart

He's knocking on the door of your heart.
He's knocking on the door of your heart.
He's knocking on the door of your heart.
He's waiting like a gentleman.

He's knocking on the door of your heart.
He's knocking on the door of your heart.
He's knocking on the door of your heart.
He's waiting for you to let Him in.

Now, peace, joy, forgiveness:
He wants to give you all of this.
Now, grace, love, and kindness.
He is the Root of David.

He's knocking on the door of your heart.
He's knocking on the door of your heart.
He's knocking on the door of your heart.
He's waiting like a gentleman.

He's knocking on the door of your heart.
He's knocking on the door of your heart.
He's knocking on the door of your heart.
He's waiting for you to let Him in.

Now, faith, hope, and healing
He wants to make His dwelling.
His Life, His Word unending.
He is the perfect blessing.

He's knocking on the door of your heart.
He's knocking on the door of your heart.
He's knocking on the door of your heart.
He's waiting like a gentleman.

He's knocking on the door of your heart.
He's knocking on the door of your heart.
He's knocking on the door of your heart.
He's waiting for you to let Him in.

Application

Perhaps you have felt the need to toughen yourself to survive in this world. You have gone through a lot, more than you think anyone can ever understand. You have learned to wear a mask around your heart to protect yourself from harm. In this manner, you believe that no one can hurt you.

You might be a single mom who has been abandoned and discredited, in more ways than one.

You might be a woman who has walked hot cement streets on her bare feet for years.

You might have been mistreated or called names that hurt you deeply.

You might have been in an accident or suffered a terrible tragedy.

Or ...

You might be a young girl or young woman like I was: wounded by the hurts and disappointments of her past. Your mind, heart, body, and soul have been misused and abused by people, the world, yourself, or the enemy.

"The Lord is merciful and gracious, slow to anger and abounding in steadfast love" (Psalm 103:8). He sees your heart and wants to dwell with you. He loves you like no one else in the world ever could, and He understands you on a level you cannot even understand yourself. He died for you, and He knows pain, sorrow, and suffering. He wants to give you Himself. He wants to soften your heart with His forgiveness, kindness, love, and generosity. He wants to fill your heart so you are overflowing with His goodness. As you trust in Him, He can satisfy you and make you more like Him.

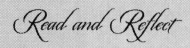

Romans 6:5: How are we united with Christ?

_____

_____

_____

_____

_____

_____

_____

Galatians 3:26–27: What are we called to do when we are baptized into Christ?

_____

_____

_____

_____

_____

_____

_____

Ephesians 5:31–32: What is the great mystery Paul speaks of?

_____

_____

_____

_____

_____

_____

_____

_____

Writing His Story on Your Heart

In every story, there are characters. There are good and bad characters, protagonists and antagonists. In His story, the protagonist is Jesus Christ. He is the hero of humankind, as He came to save us from our sins. The character of Jesus Christ is good, and if you receive Him as your Lord and Savior, you are promised a happy ending, eternal life with Him. You're promised the Holy Spirit, Who will give you the power to obey God while you're here. The antagonist in His story is Satan, who comes to kill, steal, and destroy our minds, hearts, and bodies. His character is evil. He is constantly tempting us to sin and disobey God. If we do not repent and we die in our sins, we will go to hell. This is a sad ending.

Unlike so many stories that are communicated through books, movies, and TV shows, God's story is a true love story. God loves us unconditionally in our sins and desires to be in fellowship with us. Jesus came to earth to set our captive hearts free. He does not want us to be enslaved to the powers of sin and darkness. He wants us to be able to freely love Him back, and the only way we can do this is by obeying Him, step by step. He helps us to trust Him, as our hero, Savior, and lover of our souls. When we do, we are liberated to serve God and others around us. He is true, eternal life. This is why Jesus came to earth and died on the cross—so we can have unhindered fellowship with our Creator, Maker, and Father again.

For those He saves, Jesus changes our character. The Bible says the character of the old person in us can only bear the fruit of death (Romans 7). Because of our old fallen nature, we are prone to sin and disobey God's will. If you take a look around the world now, men and women are affected by sin in some way or another. Under the influence of the power of sin and darkness, we commit wrongful acts that are an abomination in God's sight. There are "six things that the Lord hates, seven that are an abomination to him: haughty eyes, a lying tongue, and hands that shed innocent blood, a heart that devises wicked plans, feet that make haste to run to evil, a false witness who breathes out lies, and one who sows discord among brothers" (Proverbs 6:16–19). This is much of humanity today.

The character of the new believer is Christ-like (Colossians 3). Romans 6:22 says, "But now that you have been set free from sin and have become slaves of God, the fruit you get leads to sanctification and its end, eternal life." New believers in Christ are being transformed into His image, denying their own will and choosing to do God's will, which is good. Unlike actors in a play, we cannot pretend to be a character in His story. Rather, God Himself works in us by His Holy Spirit to give us the desire to do what pleases Him. As we obey Him, our lives are truly changed, and we get to shine for Him. We become a part of His story forever.

Looking back on my own past, I played a thief, a sorcerer, and an adulterer in His story. I was evil and corrupt, prone to sin against God and my neighbor. Though my outer appearance reflected a decent person, God knew my heart. He was not delighted in my sin. Over time, the Lord has called me to die to self and live to Him. As I surrender to Him, take up my cross, and follow Him, I am becoming a new person. John 1:12 says, "But to all who did receive him, who believed in his name, he gave the right to become children of God."

"But you are a chosen race, a royal priesthood, a holy nation, a people for his own possession, that you may proclaim the excellencies of him who called you out of darkness into his marvelous light" (1 Peter 2:9).

This is my identity now. I am loved, blessed, chosen, adopted, and redeemed in Christ. I am His ambassador, messenger, and representative here on earth. I am a child of God. Jesus calls me to serve—to give, forgive, bless, and rescue others around me. He commands me to love Him with all of my heart, soul, mind, and strength and to love my neighbor as myself. This character is who God created me to be all along, and I cannot be this person without Him. Without Him, I can do nothing (John 15:5). I can do all things through Christ who strengthens me and all things are possible with Him (Philippians 4:13; Matthew 19:26). I need His Living Word in me and help by His Holy Spirit to move me forward in His likeness. The Bible says that His story is alive and active in us today. He is the bright and morning star. His story is all about Him, and it is written for His glory.

Being a part of His living story is better, He has shown me, than being on any world stage. The former is for His glory and is eternal; everyone is pointed to Him as we live and move and have our being in Him. The latter is for the glory of self; everyone mourns at the end of a life of meaninglessness. No one remembers what is but a vapor.

But His name—the name of Jesus is the name that is above all names and will be remembered forever.

"Your name, O Lord, endures forever, your renown, O Lord, throughout all ages" (Psalm 135:13).

Reflecting the Artist

When we've played a role in our lives for so long, it can be hard for us to change.

The Bible says we cannot change by ourselves, even if we have the best intentions.

We need the power of the Holy Spirit to work in our hearts to change us, to help us become the people we were created to be here.

After one long night with God, I thought I might never see the light of day again. I felt like I died on my bedroom floor, and I did not know what would happen after this time.

I did not even know I could get up from this place, until I did.

Eventually, I got up from the ground where I laid, and walked into my bathroom at the time.

God led me there. He nudged me to look in the mirror. When I did, I felt me fading away. Darkness was dying. The person who I once was lost power—I died. God's power was rising in me. He was stripping me of everything false, and I could feel it. The new person in me was becoming alive in Christ.

Our identity in Christ is true.

The rest of who we think we are is a lie.

It fades. It is fading.

As I saw a reflection in the mirror, I thought about a scripture, 1 Corinthians 13:12–13: "For now we see in a mirror dimly, but then face to face. Now I know in part; then I shall know fully, even as I have been fully known. So now faith, hope, and love abide, these three; but the greatest of these is love."

That early morning, faith, hope, and love arose in me. I could see them in the mirror now. They were alive and real.

I do not know what kind of struggles you have had in knowing your identity in Christ. Because of our past, we often function from a place of deception. We walk according to who we were in the world or who others said we are now. These impressions affect our hearts. We battle to know and live out who we are called to be as Christ's ambassadors here on earth. I know what that is like, and I want to assure you that God's Word is far more powerful than any lie we believe about Him or ourselves. His Word is far greater than what others say or think about us. Even if people around us have false expectations of us, we need not live according to their perceptions of us.

Sometimes, we do. Not because we want to but because we do not yet believe what God says about us.

The truth is, because of who Jesus Christ is and what He has done for us on the cross, He defines our identity and future. It does not matter what I say or anyone else says about me. He is right. He is true. He is forever. Think on these things (Philippians 4:8).

I pray that we would know our identity in Christ, who He says we are, so that we might press forward onto the upward call that is in Christ Jesus (Philippians 3:14).

Remember the voice of God is what matters, not anyone else's opinion. The Master Artist is in charge of what He is making, shaping, and creating for His glory.

So all that will be seen and glorified in us will be His Son, the star, the hero of His story.

The Master Artist

My fingers. I am His creation, unable to go to sleep without reminding the world that life can only be found in Him. So I write.
He is our Creator.
He is the Master Artist.
He gives us breath.
Look at the creases on your palm and the fissures on your tongue. You are a miracle, conceived by a Living Designer.

My lips. They want to make Him famous. Unable to tell of His person without being mocked, I am shocked. But it doesn't matter.
He is God.
He is already the ultimate hero.
He commands His armies.
See the mountains and the seas, the stars and the trees.
You are but dust, made in His image. He knows you.

My feet. They need a place to rest. Unable to leave my room without Him filling me afresh, I wait for His Living Water. I am desperate.
He is our Daily Bread.
He is the Sustainer.
He offers us His blood to drink.
Hear His Holy Spirit speak, and bring you to your knees. You are a soul, in need of a loving Savior.

My eyes. They exist to seek His face. Unable to accept the empty promises of the world, I cling to His Word. It is forever.
He is my Bridegroom.
He is the faithful Maker.
He pours Himself out unto death on the cross.
Feel the beat of your heart, and respond to Him knocking.
In Him, you are forgiven, accepted in the Beloved.

My body. He dwells in me. Unable to find satisfaction
in the counterfeit story, I choose to walk with Him and
move from glory to glory. It is a dream come true.
These fingers. Our fingers.
These lips. Our lips.
These eyes. Our eyes.
This heart. Our hearts.
I surrender. We surrender.
Believers.
We are one in Him.
Jesus.
Our Lord, our Master.
Adonai.
We become parts of His Body.
Our King, our Head.
We are members of God's household.
Elohim.
We are adopted into His family.
His story.

 **Application**

Have you ever watched a performance with these types of characters? Who are you in His story? Do you feel you have a captive heart? Do you feel enslaved to your sin and desire to be rescued by Jesus Christ, the hero of humankind? He loves you indefinitely and longs to save you. Are you willing to admit you need Him? Are you willing to leave your sins and follow Him? Are you willing to pursue God's will for your life, so that you can be a part of His eternal love story? So you can be with Him forever and ever, in heaven? God may be speaking to your heart now, and all you need to do is respond to His unconditional love for you. Jesus died for all of your sins on the cross more than two thousand years ago, and believing in Him can give you a new name, nature, and role in Him, in His story.

Read and Reflect

Revelation 22:16: What does the angel testify?

_____

_____

_____

_____

_____

_____

_____

Colossians 3:1–17: What are we called to seek? How can we continue to live as God has called us to live here?

_____

_____

_____

_____

_____

_____

_____

Ephesians 1: What does Paul say the saints of Ephesus are blessed with?

_____

_____

_____

_____

_____

_____

_____

Reshaping Your Heart

A silhouette is a likeness cut from dark material and mounted on a light background. It is the image of a person represented as a solid shape of a single color. When a silhouette is against a sunset, its image casts a shadow.

In art class one day, our students cut out the shape of a butterfly with black material. Placing it against a sunset, the shape of the butterfly reflected darkness. The contrast between the dark butterfly and sunset background was evident. I wondered what the butterfly would look like if the light of the sun shined on it.

As one of our art students painted her sunset, she called me to help her. She tried her best to pronounce my name, and I did not mind that it came out, "Chrysala." My name sounded like "Chrysala," anyway.

I felt God speak to my heart, saying, "You're in a chrysalis right now."

A chrysalis is the hardened outer layer of a pupa. It is the sheltered stage of growth before the pupa transforms into a butterfly. In this stage, "the tissue, limbs and organs of the caterpillar transform."[15] The caterpillar is hidden, morphing. It is changing and being shaped into what it was created to become—a butterfly.

As I observed my art students painting their sunset, I noticed one of them stroking her paintbrush in different directions. Her brush moved upward and then straight across her paper, resulting in an awkward picture of the sunset. She had such a hard time painting in one direction because she was accustomed to old habits of painting in many different directions. I took her hand and helped her see the importance of painting in one direction—moving in one way only.

God whispered to my heart again, "Follow Me." I felt the Lord's tug for me to become mature in Christ, like an adult butterfly, a new creation in the shelter of His wings. He was still changing me, reshaping me, and helping me to walk consistently in His ways.

The Bible says, "But seek first the kingdom of God and his righteousness, and all these things will be added to you" (Matthew 6:33). "Jesus said to him, 'I am the way, and the truth, and the life. No one comes to the Father except through me'" (John 14:6). John 10:10 says, "The thief comes only to steal and kill and destroy. I come that they may have life and have it abundantly."

The longer we practice our old habits, the more opportunities we give to the enemy to rob us from our new life in Christ. Our new life in Christ is God's best for us. It is His will for our lives.

I knew in that moment that God wanted me to walk in His ways in every area of my life. I could no longer walk like a child and go to the left or right. I needed to align myself totally to His Heart. When we do this, we can live an abundant life in Him on a consistent basis.

---

[15] https://www.natgeokids.com/uk/discover/animals/insects/butterfly-life-cycle/.

We can fly where He directs us. Through His life, we can impact the dying world around us. If we are in a chrysalis stage of development with Christ, we can submit to His call to be reshaped in His ways. In this manner, we can prepare to morph into the colorful butterfly He ultimately is shaping us to be here.

Seeing Like the Artist

More than ever, I started to see that the Master Artist sees differently than we do.

In order to fulfill His will in our lives, we need to believe in His promises.

Sometimes, all we have are His promises.

"For nothing will be impossible with God" (Luke 1:37). This was a scripture that was impressed upon my heart as I was morphing, changing, and transitioning into a new season of my journey with God.

I started to recognize that truly, I am nothing. I am nothing but a testimony of the grace of God in my life.

I needed to start walking by faith, not by sight.

True artists, God's artists, do everything by faith.

Seeing through the eyes of faith, God whispered to my heart, was seeing like Him.

As artists, most of us want visuals.

I want to be sure when doubt or fear creep into my heart that God is with me. When I make mistakes that would cause the average person to give up on me, I want to be sure that God will not leave me. When my task seems too big for me to take on alone, I want to know that God will carry me through it.

2 Corinthians 1:20 says, "For all the promises of God find their Yes *in* him. That is why it is through him that we utter our Amen to God for his glory."

God is faithful to His Word.

He is Who He says He is, and sometimes, we simply need to believe.

I needed to see like He saw; He saw the depths of my heart from the very beginning and pursued me.

I knew that He was calling me to look at the hearts of those He wanted me to pour into for His glory.

I needed to believe Him and see through His eyes.

He looks at the human heart and chooses to love, to serve.

A Child of the King

The devil mocks me, but he can't hurt me anymore.
I stand on God's Word, who He says I am, forevermore.
I'm a child of the King, hidden in His love,
forgiven and redeemed, secured in Him above.

I wear the belt of truth and choose to proclaim His name.
Jesus Christ, my strength and savior—I'm not ashamed.
When the devil mocks me, I reach for the sword.
When I'm weak and weary, I cry out to the Lord.

This world tries to distract me and pull me from the mission,
from the heavenly command, to preach the Gospel to all creation.
There's only one way to God: through Jesus Christ, His Son.
There's only one way to heaven: to believe in Him and repent.

I confess to the Lord, I lost sight of the vision
to use all I have for His everlasting Kingdom.
The grass withers, and the flower fades.
The Word of the Lord stands forever; His will remains.

Stored up in me, He desires His way
to share His good news with all who've gone astray.
His message of peace is simple and sweet.
God is good and merciful; He forgives the meek.

Help me, O Lord, to redeem the time,
to serve and to bless, to steward and invest.
Every moment is Yours to use for Your glory.
Every cell, every gift, to share with Your Body.

The devil tries to mock me, but I'm not going to stop.
I'm jumping back in the race; I'm running after God's Heart.
The devil tries to condemn me, but I'm not going to listen.
I'm turning to the Lord and claiming my identity in Him.

The world is passing away, and everything in it.
The one who does the will of the Father will abide forever.
I'm listening for His voice; I'm waiting on His best
to press on towards the upward calling in Christ Jesus.

His kingdom come, His will be done
on earth as it is in heaven. He's coming again.
I'm living for Christ; I'm pressing in.
Walking forward and pointing others to Him.

 **Application**

If we want to mature in Christ, we must grow up in the things of God. As we develop in Christ, we will undergo a metamorphosis of our shape. God will shape us to be more like Jesus, and we will grow into His likeness.

God desires that in this transformation of our lives, Jesus can live through us and heal others through the ministry of His beautiful Heart. "But we all, with unveiled face, beholding as in a mirror the glory of the Lord, are being transformed into the same image from glory to glory, just as from the Lord, the Spirit" (2 Corinthians 3:18 NASB). Jesus will take our weak mortal bodies and change them into glorious bodies like His own, using the same power with which He will bring everything under His control (Philippians 3:21). His beauty, like the colors of a butterfly under the light of the sun, will be shown for His glory.

Read and Reflect

2 Corinthians 3:18: Who is transforming us? What is God transforming us into?

_____
_____
_____
_____
_____
_____
_____
_____

Romans 12:2: How does God transform us? How can we discern the will of God?

_____
_____
_____
_____
_____
_____
_____

Matthew 17:2: Who did Jesus reveal Himself to? What was the disciples' response?

_____
_____
_____
_____
_____
_____
_____

Painting Your Heart

Have you ever viewed creation as a living painting? If you take a look at a flower, fruit, or a tree planted in fertile soil, you will notice a special design in each of them. As the Artist, God has a unique intention and purpose for all His creations. There is a direction in which creation grows and moves in order to fulfill its function. The Bible says that Jesus Christ is the substance and foundation of all creation. He is the source of all spiritual life. He is the true seed that gives us new life. He is the Living Water. He is the Light. He is before all things, and by Him, all things consist (Colossians 1:17). Without Him, creation can neither exist, grow, or last.

Jesus Christ is the Word of God, and He calls us to be found in Him. We must build our lives upon Him and make Him the center of everything we do. This is one of the reasons He says we should have no other gods before Him. If He is not the leading root of the decisions we make in our lives, we will not bloom. How can we ever grow and function in the way He purposed unless we follow our Creator's commands? We need to be grounded in Jesus Christ and obey Him so we can bear good fruit (John 15:1–8). When we do, we can have an abundant life in Him, existing and living for what we were created for—His glory. We can fulfill our function in the Body of Christ and rest in Who He is to us: our Head (Colossians 1:18). For we live and move and have our being in Him (Acts 17:28).

If you paint a rose, you will want to paint its petals in the direction they are growing, right? If you stroke your paintbrush upward and sideways on one petal, for example, you will reflect disorder. Your rose will look a little funny. Similarly, we as God's Art must go in the direction the Holy Spirit is leading us. God gives His Holy Spirit to help us obey Him and be in harmony with His plan for us. God is a God of order—He has a distinct design and purpose for His Art. We must be controlled by the Holy Spirit rather than our own will.

While helping one of my art students paint a rose one day, I heard her grandmother comment to me, "You are so patient. Where did you learn that from? Art school?"

I reflected on her question. I chuckled. *What?* I thought. *I didn't even go to art school.*

God, You are so good, I thought. *I learned how to be like this from You.*

"I was trained here at this art studio," I said, "under my boss."

God whispered to my heart, "You were trained under my Spirit." Immediately, I glorified God in my heart. *Glory to you, God! Thank you, Lord!*

I looked back at my student's grandmother and smiled gently at her; I said, "It's not me. It's the Lord."

The patience she witnessed came from the source of patience. It came from the Holy Spirit. He is patient. He is patient in teaching me to do His will (Psalm 25:4–5, 27:11, 86:11). God was pleased, and I felt His delight touch the center of my heart. It was wonderful. Like an artist who takes pleasure in his creation, I felt God's enjoyment. When we remain in Christ, I learned, we reflect Him without even using words. He is Who He is, and we were made for His glory.

My Artist is painting a big picture we cannot fully perceive on earth. His fruit—His character—His Heart is pounding through His love, patience, kindness, and gentleness for people, and more. He desires our redemption in Him. He is the light of the world, shining and displaying His beauty to all.

The brightness of His glory, I want to follow—hear, taste, and experience forever.

Do you?

If you are in Christ, you are a part of His beautiful masterpiece too. If you would like to be in Him, you can open your heart to Him and answer His sweet calling now.

Join Him.
Follow Him.
Die with Him.
Live unto Him.
Serve Him.
He is worth it all.

Being in the Artist

One day, God asked me to trust Him with my future.

Where did He want me to fly, to serve Him next?

I knew a chapter in my story had ended, and He was moving me along, to a new place.

Redemption was here now, in me because of Jesus. Because of His death on the cross and His resurrection from the grave, I was with Him now.

Where are we going? I wondered.

I was in a new life with Him.

It was as if my reality no longer fit what was growing deep within me.

"Go." I heard God's call. *Go where?*

His calling was becoming so strong in me, stronger than the voices around me, pressuring me to do something I knew I was not created to do. These other voices were sweet but distracting. They were not interested in having me fulfill God's calling on my life.

God was. He was the God of my past and my present, and after many more battles, I knew He is the God of my future.

If I believed He was my Creator, I also needed to believe that He created me to do something specific. I was *His* new creation, wasn't I?

With the help of His Word, God helped me to trust that He would open a new door for me to serve Him.

Shortly after I made my decision to take a leap of faith in Christ, He did.

I left my job at the art studio. It was time for me to do so. He opened a new door for me to become the art teacher at a Christian school.

When I was hired, I was told that there had been no art at this school years ago. A few years prior, they decided to start an art program.

God whispered to my heart at this time, "I redeemed your heart. This is where I'm calling you to serve me now."

This was His school, and He was inviting me to do His work—in His Kingdom for His glory at this place. For hearts. He wanted me to engage and be a part of Kingdom education, truly creative education. Through art, He wanted to draw children to Himself—to His Heart. To paint a new life in them, like He did for me.

When I first walked into the Art Room, I entered an empty space. It was very different from the vision God placed in my heart. Except there was one bright, orange flower painted on the back wall of the sliding doors. It was almost recognizable—like He already painted this picture in my heart.

It was blooming and rising, as if the sun was shining on it. Someone painted it there before I came. Alongside the flower was the scripture, "For God gave us a spirit not of fear but of power and love and self-control" (2 Timothy 1:7).

Seeing His hand upon this place, I cried and cried before the Lord. I felt overwhelmed by His grace.

God eventually restored this room. All of what He gave me to me throughout the years of healing my own heart, He poured out onto the walls of the room. The walls were painted white to remind us that we are His Bride. The borders in the room were painted turquoise to remind us of the sanctification He offers to us. The borders of the windows were painted purple to remind us that Jesus is our King, and we are a part of His royal lineage. A bookshelf was donated to us and we painted it pink to remind us of being in a right relationship with God. On the back sliding doors, my friend and I painted more flowers; a garden began to grow. Children entered the room, and God began to show me His Heart for them.

These were the days I realized how much bigger God's dreams were than my own. His vision requires a sacrifice, a denial of self for others.

I felt like a mere paintbrush in the Artist's hand, as I did whatever He told me to do. But I never felt so fulfilled, as He had His way in and through me.

"But now thus says the Lord, he who created you, O Jacob, he who formed you, O Israel: 'Fear not, for I have redeemed you; I have called you by name, you are mine'" (Isaiah 43:1).

I was completely stunned.

God had a plan. He is faithful.

And He continues His faithfulness.

The Artist will have His way with His heartwork and what He desires to do in and through us.

A Paintbrush in the Artist's Hand

I am a paintbrush in the Artist's hand,
abiding in His gracious plan.
He washes me with Living Water.
He rinses away any hardened plaster.

I am a paintbrush in the Artist's hand,
flowing in His simple command.
He softens every toughened bristle.
He restores in me a living epistle.

His Heart.
His beauty.
He's the Artist of humanity.
His Heart.
His beauty.
He's all the light we need.

I am a paintbrush in the Artist's hand,
trusting in His sovereign plan.
He dips me in bright colors.
He paints a new life in service to others.

Revealing tints and tones of forgiveness
highlighting His mercy, love, and goodness,
making me a part of His royal lineage,
transforming me into His humble image.

I am a paintbrush in the Artist's hand,
longing to reflect more of His divine plan.
His vision for the masterpiece, I need not question.
His desire for creation, I know is redemption.

His Heart.
His beauty.
He's all I want to see.
His Heart.
His life.
He's all the love we need.

His Heart.
His beauty.
He's all I need to see.
His Heart.
His life.
He's all the light we need.

Jesus.
You're the Artist of the broken soul.
Jesus.
You're the peace Who makes us whole.
Jesus.
Shine your light on every shattered part.
Jesus.
Take our pieces and heal our hearts.

 **Application**

I encourage you to surrender, submit, and respond to God's direction in your heart. Many voices in our minds tempt us to disobey His leading and calling on our lives. There is the enemy's voice, our voice, and God's voice. When we do not listen to the Master Artist's voice, He is displeased. We can cry out to Him to deliver us from evil, and He is faithful.

If you are in a situation that God is not pleased with right now, call on the name of Jesus. Repent of your choice to listen to this strange voice over your Creator's voice, and flee from your sin. "So flee youthful passions and pursue righteousness, faith, love, and peace, along with those who call on the Lord from a pure heart" (2 Timothy 2:22). Ask God to forgive you and help you to wait on His direction so you can follow Him and only Him (John 10:27). "For my thoughts are not your thoughts, neither are your ways my ways, declares the Lord" (Isaiah 55:8).

 Read and Reflect

Ephesians 3:17: What does Paul pray that we are rooted and grounded in?

_____
_____
_____
_____
_____
_____
_____
_____

Romans 8: Who is no longer condemned? Why?

_____
_____
_____
_____
_____
_____
_____
_____

Galatians 5:22-23: What is the fruit of the Spirit? How can we bear this fruit?

_____
_____
_____
_____
_____
_____
_____
_____

Remaking Your Heart

In the beginning, God made Adam from the earth, from dust.

For fellowship purposes, God made a beautiful woman named Eve for Adam, from his body. Eve was made from his rib, and God made her to be his wife.

Then, God brought her to Adam.

"So the Lord God caused a deep sleep to fall upon the man, and while he slept took one of his ribs and closed up its place with flesh. And the rib that the Lord God had taken from the man he made into a woman and brought her to the man" (Genesis 2:21–22).

Genesis 2:23 says, "Then the man said, 'This at last is bone of my bones and flesh of my flesh; she shall be called Woman, because she was taken out of Man.'"

Trust and love existed between the Creator and His creation.

Then, sin came into the picture.

When sin entered the hearts of Adam and Eve, trust between the Creator and His creation was broken. Trust between Adam and Eve was violated. They fell out of the love of God in Christ Jesus by the Holy Spirit—His pure, holy, and safe presence. The eyes of their hearts were closed, ashamed of what they had done before their Creator. Darkened. Their bodies hid.

Even though they fell from there, from His love, God's love in Christ Jesus by the Holy Spirit came to revive us. His love came to heal, restore, and redeem His creation.

Trust in God, in His love, is restored through His Son, Jesus Christ.

At the cross.

We all have a story, a past of shame and guilt. In His story, we learn that humankind falls short of God's glory, His love. We need God's grace.

Abel and Abraham's offerings were a shadow of the things to come— copies of a heavenly pattern. Their acts of obedience to the Lord were a shadow of the love of God in Christ Jesus to come into the world.

The fellowship between God the Father, Son, and Holy Spirit in heaven was perfect. In His love, God the Father gave His only Son to die on the cross for us. "Although He was a Son, He learned obedience from the things which He suffered" (Hebrews 5:8 NASB). Jesus' blood is the only offering for the forgiveness of our sins that is an acceptable sacrifice in God's sight. Jesus' life was given voluntarily for the sins of the world. He had the power in His life to raise Himself up.

Jesus is called the Second Adam. He is from above, not from the earth. "In the beginning was the Word, and the Word was with God, and the Word was God. He was in the beginning with God. All things were made through him, and without him was not any thing made that was made. In him was life, and the life was the light of men" (John 1:1–4). The first man was from the earth, a man of dust; the second man is from heaven (1 Corinthians 15:47). Jesus is the eternal Word of God became flesh. His love came to this place, earth, where we lived in shame and guilt. He comes to these places in our hearts, where we can be found in Him.

The eternal Word of God became flesh to die on the cross for sinners. God's love in Christ is expansive. We can trust, receive, and be found in His love.

God calls us, the church, Jesus' Bride. Like He made Eve from Adam, God remakes us in Christ. We are joined to Him and become a part of His body. We become one flesh.

As wise, creative hearts, we must submit to the Master Artist as He makes us new, beautiful, and pure for our Bridegroom. We can make ourselves ready for His coming. We can ask God to prepare us for our heavenly home with Him. Then, our hearts can cry out to God. "The Spirit and the Bride say, 'Come.' And let the one who hears say, 'Come.' And let the one who is thirsty come; let the one who desires take the water of life without price" (Revelation 22:17).

Back in His love, the eyes of our hearts are opened, unashamed, and blameless before our Creator. Truly enlightened. We are One in Him.

For the creative heart, Jesus' blood covers your sins. His love forgives you. His love adores you. His love finds you. His love gives you a new name. You are who He says you are because of Who He is and what He has done for you on the cross.

Free. Redeemed. Healed. His precious creation and work of heart. His Bride.

If you feel broken inside, remember He will make everything beautiful in its time (Ecclesiastes 3:11).

Trust Him.

He knows the depths of what your creative heart needs—His love.

"For I am sure that neither death nor life, nor angels nor rulers, nor things present nor things to come, nor powers, nor height nor depth, nor anything else in all creation, will be able to separate us from the love of God in Christ Jesus our Lord" (Romans 8:38–39).

He gives us the choice to love and obey Him in return, to surrender, follow, see, and know Him as we are known.

Knowing the Artist

God.

He is more than I am writing; more than I am thinking; more than I am receiving.

I wonder what heaven will be like; there will be more of Him to know for eternity. That is an unfathomable concept.

Are we seeking Him here as much as we will embrace Him there?

Heaven has been my home since God created me in my mother's womb.

Yes, I was separated from God. Yes, I was far away from Him. Yes, I was lost.

He knew it.

I sought answers in other places—other religions, men, and activities.

But none of these things could fill the empty void in my heart, where God set eternity.

In rebellion, He rescued me.

The cross.

God's love.

I do not know why He bought a broken soul like me, but His Heart thought I was still worth His life.

Because of Who He is and what He did on the cross, Jesus redeemed my heart.

I am a nobody. Yet He chose to call me His—His *poiema*, His daughter, His bride.

I became His heartwork.

His love drew me back, back to Himself.

He continues to draw me, every day, even in those places where I often want to run away.

God breaks, molds, shapes, and cuts. It hurts. But I know the Artist is restoring and removing layers of deception the world once imposed upon His Art.

Now, I want Him. I want our hearts to be one all the time.

Now I see that my heart was created to be a place of worship for God.

This must be why I feel most at home when I am simply knowing Him; worshiping Him; serving Him—when we are in communion, laughing with each other, and communicating with each other. In Christ, I am understood, accepted, and known. I can relax and be His and no one else's. I do not know how foreign idols interrupt and take the place of my God.

In Christ, we are whole and complete (Colossians 2:10).

He is ...

There. Here.

Am I believing? Surrendering? Seeing? Knowing?

Are you believing? Surrendering? Seeing? Knowing?

If you haven't yet, let God draw you with His love.

He is the Master Artist.

Give Him the pencil, the clay, the paint you thought you owned. It all belongs to Him. He knows how to create a picture of true love in your heart.

Love knows how to pick up the pieces of a broken soul. Love knows how to mend and bind what has been torn apart by the destroyer. Love knows how to rip off the phony and make something genuine.

Love knows how to tenderly feed, nourish, and water beautiful flowers in Him.

Christ holds us together.

Love bears all things, believes all things, hopes all things, endures all things. Love never ends (1 Corinthians 13:7-8).

A Part of His Heartwork

From broken to beautiful,
He wants us to know
how much He loves His heartwork.
He's faithful to show.

While we were yet sinners,
while we walked in the night,
Christ came to die on the cross for us.
He came as a light.

From mourning to joy,
He writes a new story.
He lifts us from the pit.
He redeems us for His glory.

While we were yet scorners,
while we ignored Him,
Christ came to forgive His enemies.
He came as a ransom.

From heartache to fullness,
He binds up our wounds.
He gives us His peace.
He gives us good news.

We are a part of His heartwork.
He won't leave us undone.
He'll never leave us nor forsake us.
He'll be with us til the end.

Let Him write His Word on your heart.
Let Him sing you psalms.
Let Him draw you with gentle cords
and find rest in His loving arms.

The darkness will become a fading memory.
The light will hold you still,
reflecting all your blind spots
He'll make you a glorious seal.

Upon His Heart, you'll be impressed.
Upon His Heart, you'll see His love
transformed into His image,
remade in Him above.

Walking with your Creator,
it's a joy to see Him move.
Talking with your Maker,
you'll feel His Heart for the ordinary few.

He sits with the brokenhearted.
He picks up the fallen.
He listens to the bitter soul.
He finds the forgotten.

His heartwork
He completes.
His story,
He redeems.

Humble, He is.
The beautiful Prince of Peace.

 **Application**

I'd like to invite you to say another prayer with me, in your heart.

Father God, I ask that You please open the eyes of my heart. Open the eyes of all of Your creative hearts, that we may see You. Search us and know us. Find us, Jesus. Heal the sick. Open the eyes of the blind. Let the deaf hear. Set the captives free. Great Physician; Good Samaritan, please take the plank out of our own eyes and help us to see, breathe, and receive Your love. Keep us in Your light. Help us to live in Your love and to never walk away from it. To abide in it. To stay there, with You. Here, where we can trust and know You more and more. In Jesus' name. Amen.

Genesis 2:22–24: How did God make a woman?

_____
_____
_____
_____
_____
_____
_____
_____

Ephesians 5:22–33: Who is the head of the wife? Who is the head of the church?

_____
_____
_____
_____
_____
_____
_____

Romans 6:5–14: How are we united with Christ in His death and resurrection?

_____
_____
_____
_____
_____
_____
_____

That if you confess with your mouth the Lord Jesus and believe in your heart that God has raised Him from the dead, you will be saved.

Romans 10:9